101 MORE ITEMS TO SELL ON EBAY

101 MORE ITEMS TO SELL ON EBAY

Learn How To Make Money Reselling Garage Sale & Thrift Store Finds

ANN ECKHART

101 MORE ITEMS TO SELL ON EBAY

The sequel to the highly successful book "101 Items to Sell on Ebay: How to Make Money Selling Garage Sale & Thrift Store Finds" By Ann Eckhart

INTRODUCTION

I started selling on Ebay in 2005, first using the site to liquidate excess inventory from my home-based gift basket business before changing my business model to sell new gift products (ceramics, plush toys, books) on both Ebay and Amazon. Along the way, I began teaching others how to sell on Ebay through videos on my YouTube channel; and in 2013, I started writing books about how to make money on Ebay.

My very first book, "101 Items to Sell on Ebay: How to Make Money Selling Garage Sale & Thrift Store Finds!" remains one of my best-selling books to date. That book's success has prompted me to follow up with this sequel, "101 MORE Items to Sell on Ebay!"; I hope that it proves just as helpful to fellow Ebay sellers as the first volume has been!

Since I started "picking" (or "reselling," as I prefer to call it) items up at garage sales, estate sales, and thrift stores to resell on Ebay, the number one question I continually get asked is, "What items sell on Ebay?" This is a loaded question if there ever was one as almost anything has sold or can sell on the online auction site. However, fads come and go; while Beanie Babies were once hot, you now cannot give them away. And while some items in a particular category may sell online, not everything will. For instance, SOME coffee mugs sell well on Ebay. However, MOST coffee mugs do not.

In fact, the vast majority of things you find secondhand will not sell on Ebay, whether it is due to the product being in poor condition or just not being desirable to anyone. There is a lot of "Made in China" junk out there; being a successful Ebay seller is all about learning how to find the few items that will sell among the vast amounts of merchandise that will not. This is a skill that takes time to develop, and even now, I still pick up duds that end up not being worth anything on Ebay.

In my first book and now in this one, I share my personal go-to items, which I have been picking up and reselling on Ebay for years. These are all realistic items that most anyone can find secondhand in their area. This is NOT a get-rich-quick book. This is a book filled with items that sell on Ebay anywhere from $10 to $100. None of these things are going to let you retire early, but selling a combination of them will definitely add to your bank account!

Every single item I list in this book is one I have personally sold. I provide you with a description of each item and what to look for, and in many cases, I also share what I originally paid (if I can remember!) and then what I sold it for. I also provide tips and tricks for listing as well as how to shipping.

Regardless of what you read in the following pages, however, it is up to you to do your research when listing anything for sale on Ebay. Conditions and prices are always changing, so be sure to do a completed listing search to see what an item recently sold for before pricing yours. Perhaps an item listed in this book may currently not be selling as well, or it might be going for much MORE than I made.

Bottom line: Always do your research! While the active Ebay listings show what buyers are ASKING for their items, the completed listings show what, if anything, they actually sold for. Items are only worth what someone is willing to pay!

On Ebay, it is not just about having the right items to sell, though. You need to have a keyword-loaded title, great photos (and lots of them!), a detailed description, and professional customer service policies. And after the sale has been made, you then need to package your merchandise and ship it out quickly. Take the time to do each step in the listing and shipping process correctly, and you will significantly cut down on customer complaints and returns, which in turn will keep you in good standing on Ebay so that you can continue selling.

It is essential to recognize the fact that Ebay is not YOUR business, but rather a TOOL you use in selling online. To make money on Ebay, you need to follow their policies and guidelines. And it really is simple: describe your items accurately, package them professionally, and ship them out quickly. The right items, plus great listings, plus excellent customer service, all add to you being a successful Ebay seller! And with the items listed in this book, you will be on your way to tackling the first requirement for making money on Ebay, which is to have sellable products.

And now, here are 101 MORE items that you can find at garage sales and thrift stores to resell on Ebay!

101 MORE ITEMS TO SELL ON EBAY

(In Alphabetical Order)

#1 ADVERTISING & PROMOTIONAL ITEMS

Have you ever been to a garage sale or thrift store and spotted a coffee mug with a product or company logo on it? "Who would want such a thing?" you may have asked yourself. Well, plenty of people out there collect advertising promotional pieces, so these are always great items to pick up!

For example, I have sold a plush yellow duck advertising Duck brand packing tape for $15 as well as coffee mugs with corporate logos on them for $10. Products from companies no longer in business or that have undergone name changes are almost always fast sellers on Ebay. I have found Apple promotional pieces with the old "Macintosh" name and logo on them that sold within minutes of me listing them.

I have also sold pens, pins, buttons, bags, hats, belt buckles, awards, and trophies branded with various corporate logos, in addition to plush toys and coffee mugs. Since these items only sell to particular buyers (usually not the people attending the garage sale they are being sold at), they are often the last items left on the last day of the sale. Therefore, I can usually pick up advertising pieces for as little as a quarter.

Do not think of these advertising items as things people will USE but instead as pieces that they COLLECT. Promotional products from brands and corporations are usually cheap to pick up, and they make great additions to your Ebay store. People are often searching for these items because their parents or they themselves worked there. So, you are selling a memory more than a functional product.

Ebay has an entire "Collectibles" category on their site, which you can then narrow down into sub-categories, one of which is "Advertising." While the name of the company printed on the item you want to sell may not be in one of the subcategories (as an example, "Coca-Cola" is a subcategory under "Soda"; but there is also an "Other" choice for pop brands not listed), try to narrow down your item as best you can into as many sub-categories as possible (i.e., Don't just select "Collectibles" and then "Other"; try to find a subcategory it can be listed under).

As with everything I list on Ebay, providing multiple clear photographs is essential in getting top dollar. Since advertising pieces tend to have a small following, I list these at Fixed Price as there usually are not enough people who want them to bid them up at auction. Plus, it can sometimes take a while for the right buyer for these pieces to come along.

And since brands and companies are globally recognized, be sure to open up your listings to international buyers. Ebay's Global Shipping Program makes selling to overseas customers a breeze. When an Ebay customer purchases something in the Global Shipping Program, the mailing address is automatically changed to that of Ebay's processing center in Kentucky. You simply package the order as you usually would, and when Ebay gets the package, they will handle any relabeling or customs forms that are needed. And they also take responsibility for the package if it becomes lost or damaged.

#2 AIRLINE MERCHANDISE

Mugs, glasses, and bags from airlines, especially those that are no longer in business, are hot sellers on Ebay. Some people collect any type of aviation memorabilia, and folks who only pick up items from specific carriers. I have never been able to keep branded airline merchandise in my Ebay store for long as the items always get snatched up fast.

I have sold basic American Airlines coffee mugs for an easy $10 each, as well as an American Airlines teapot that was missing its lid for $10. I am always on the lookout for Pan Am items, especially the flight attendant's travel bags in the 1960s. I found one once, but it had been slashed to pieces. Seriously, someone took a KNIFE to it and cut it up. It broke my heart!

The reason airline merchandise sells well on Ebay is that it is pretty rare. Most pieces are only given to airline employees and are not available to the general public. Or they were serving pieces used in first-class or international flights, which meant someone likely swiped them from the plane.

Most airline merchandise is straightforward in design; china dishes are usually basic white with just the airline logo on them. While coffee mugs are the most common item to find, you also want to be on the lookout for patches (from employee uniforms), service pins (given to the flight crew), hats, bags, and even vintage brochures.

Ebay has an "Airlines" subcategory under the "Collectibles" main category; simply choose "Collectibles," "Transportation," "Aviation," and then "Airlines." You can then choose the airline carrier of the item you are listing.

#3 APPLE MACINTOSH

As I mentioned earlier, advertising and promotional pieces can sell very well on Ebay; and one name to always be on the lookout for is Apple Macintosh. When Steve Jobs introduced the first personal computer in 1984, it was named Macintosh and was under the Apple brand. As time went by, the name was shortened to simply "Mac," and since 1998, all products are now just marketed as "Apple," which has made the "Macintosh" name extremely popular with collectors.

Apple products have an almost cult-like following, meaning some people passionately collect Macintosh branded items. I am not just talking about the Mac computers themselves (although an actual vintage Apple Mac computer can bring in big bucks), but the smaller accessories and promotional items. Even something with an old Macintosh sticker on it can sell on Ebay.

I have sold very basic Macintosh coffee mugs for $15, and I am always on the lookout for anything with the vintage logo. Be on the lookout for old software, mousepads, pens, and even floppy disk holders bearing the Macintosh name.

Restored Macintosh computers can sell for thousands of dollars on Ebay. Still, even units that are not working can be pieced out and sold for parts, including the original paperwork, software, and manuals. Unless you are 100% positive that a computer is in perfect working order, please do not list it as such as a true collector will challenge you on any small problem they might find. As with all electronics, I list any computers I sell on Ebay "as is."

There is a "Vintage Computing" subcategory on Ebay located under the "Computers/Tablets & Networking" main category, which is where I list Macintosh computers, manuals, and accessories. I list collectibles such as mugs and mouse pads under the "Collectible" category using the "Computers & High Tech" subcategory under the "Advertising" subcategory.

#4 AS SEEN ON TV SKINCARE:

If you have ever sat in front of the television flipping channels, you have likely stumbled upon QVC or HSN and saw them hawking women's skincare sets from names such as Carol's Daughter, Cindy Crawford, Philosophy, or Proactive. These brands are sold on the home shopping networks, as well as at their own retail stores and on their own websites, and the sets are rather pricey. People tend to get sucked into the sales pitch and end up ordering way too much, which is why you can sometimes find them at garage sales.

These items have a fast turnaround sales rate on Ebay, especially to international customers who cannot get them in their own countries. Be careful to check the expiration dates on these products and to disclose them in your listings. While expired products will sell, they will sell at a lower price than newer ones.

Also, be sure that if any of the products are aerosols to ship them Parcel Select within the United States or First Class for international, they cannot go on planes due to the risk of explosion. We keep a wide variety of plain cardboard boxes on hand to ship items such as these that cannot go into the free Priority Mail boxes you can get from the post office. Ebay's Global Shipping Program makes it easy to ship beauty products out of the country as Ebay handles all of the customs forms and assumes all risk for the packages if they are lost or damaged.

I always do a completed listing search on any item before I list it on Ebay to see what the current selling price is. Sometimes these skincare sets are so in demand that you may want to try your luck selling them at auction; it only takes two people who want an item to start a bidding war. However, if you find the item to be selling at a consistent price, you can ensure a quick sale if you just list it Fixed Price with the Buy It Now option.

I once found expired Proactive skincare sets at a garage sale for $5 each; despite being past their sell-by date, they sold quickly on Ebay for $25 each. I disclosed the expiration date in the listing, but it did not stop people from snatching them up. Had they not been expired, they would have gone for twice as much.

Because bottles of lotion and liquids tend to be heavy, I list skincare products using calculated shipping so that the buyer pays the postage cost to have the items delivered to their zip code. If you do offer "free" shipping, add the shipping cost to the asking price. I do this by putting items in a box and weighing them on a digital scale. I then go to the USPS website and get a shipping quote using a zipcode from Hawaii, which is the furthest distance a United States Ebay customer could be from me.

To ship liquids, we place bottles into plastic Ziploc bags and then use plenty of packing paper to prevent them from moving around during transit. Failure to properly secure skincare during shipment may result in bottles cracking and product leaking out.

#5 BAKELITE PLASTIC

Bakelite was developed in the early 1900s and is one of the first forms of plastic. After World War II, Bakelite was used to make everything from utensil handles to jewelry, and the vintage appeal of these pieces means they have a great resale value on Ebay.

Besides silverware handles and jewelry, other items made with Bakelite include clocks, desk sets, game pieces (Mah Jong sets are particularly valuable!), kitchenware, and jewelry boxes. The pieces from the 1950s have the most value, not only because of the Bakelite but because of their vintage, mid-century modern look.

To determine if a piece is genuinely Bakelite and not a modern knock-off, I use one of two easy methods. The first is to use Simi chrome Polish, which is just silver polish that you can find at Walmart or Target. We keep this on hand, anyway, to polish flatware. I rub a small amount of polish onto the piece I am testing using a Q-Tip. If the Q-Tip turns yellow, then the piece is Bakelite.

If you do not have any Simi chrome polish, then Formula 409 can be used. As with the polish, if the 409 on the Q-tip or cloth turns yellow after being rubbed on the item, then the piece is Bakelite. When listing anything as Bakelite on Ebay, it is critical that you test for it using the methods I listed above. You can then put "tested positive using Simi chrome polish" in the listing to assure customers that the piece is, in fact, Bakelite. You can also put the word "tested" in the listing title.

I always look through the utensil piles at estate sales to see if there are any pieces with plastic handles. Commonly the handles are pale yellow, dull orange, or avocado green. The last Bakelite pieces I sold were a simple knife and fork set that went for $10; I had paid 25-cents for the pair. During a fill-a-bag sale, I will load up on any vintage plastic bracelets I find to test them for Bakelite.

Ebay has an entire subcategory under the "Collectibles" category for Bakelite, but you can also list in the category-specific to the item you are selling, such as jewelry. If you have done a completed listing search but still are not sure how to price your Bakelite piece, do not be afraid to try your luck with an Ebay auction. Bakelite jewelry, Mah Jong sets, and home décor pieces are so sought after by collectors that it is common for bidding wars to erupt. However, be sure to start the auction at a price you will be happy with just in case you only have one bidder.

Small Bakelite pieces are lightweight enough to ship via First Class in a bubble mailer. As with everything I list on Ebay, I weigh the item along with the box or envelope it will likely ship in beforehand so that I can put a weight into the listing. Even if I offer "free" shipping for economy, some customers will pay for expedited shipping (i.e., Priority); plus, international customers must pay the shipping cost regardless.

#6 BATH & BODY WORKS

You are probably familiar with Bath & Body Works stores, as they are in about every American shopping mall. This retailer of scented soaps and lotions is not only popular in the United States but around the world. However, not all scents are sold in every country. Therefore, selling products that are only available in YOUR country to international buyers is a great way to earn money on Ebay, especially if you get the products on clearance or unused at garage sales.

I myself have sold unwanted Bath & Body Works items many times on Ebay. Whether they were products I had gotten as a gift and did not like or were things I found cheap at a garage sale, unused Bath & Body Works products have always been a quick sale for me on Ebay.

However, don't go rushing into a Bath & Body Works store to purchase their products at full-price to resell on Ebay. As with anything you are reselling, you want to make sure to buy LOW and sell HIGH. Plus, there are already so many other sellers doing this that the competition drives down the price. I am also wary of buying these products on clearance as so many other online sellers also do this. I stick to buying Bath & Body Works secondhand at garage sales as I can usually pick them up for less than $1. However, I only buy them new and unused as Ebay prohibits the sale of used cosmetics unless they are vintage.

Because the Post Office prohibits anything liquid or potential flammable from being shipped Priority Mail (Priority Mail often goes onto the airplanes, and the altitude pressure can cause products to explode), you will need to list Bath & Body Works products via Parcel Post. We keep a wide selection of various-sized plain cardboard boxes on hand just for items such as this that we cannot ship Priority.

Due to their bulky size, bath products are almost always an item that I list using calculated shipping so that the buyer pays the postage cost to their zip code. Trying to add the weight of these heavy bottles into the price of an item to list it with "free" shipping inflates the cost to a ridiculous level. Buyers who genuinely want something will pay for shipping, so do not be afraid to list items without free shipping.

#7 BEER SIGNS

The popularity of men creating "Man Caves" in their basements and garages means that beer signs are highly sought after. Also, bars and restaurants like to add these pieces to their establishments. The more bells and whistles the sign has (lights, motion), the more money it will bring. Vintage signs with tube lights are prevalent.

Of course, finding vintage signs that are in good condition and that still work can be a challenge, and being able to pick these pieces up for a reasonable price is another challenge considering their popularity. Signs that are reasonably priced are often the first things to sell at garage and estate sales. Shipping these signs is also risky as they are fragile and can break easily.

However, if you do want to take a chance on a beer sign, be sure to test it before buying. While you may be able to simply change the bulb to make a sign work again, others may require more skill. Some buyers are willing to purchase signs that do not work, but any repairs customers have to do on their end will decrease the amount of money you can ask for.

As with everything I list on Ebay, I first do a completed listing search to see what the going price of an item is to determine if I want to list it as Fixed Price or take my chances at auction. If I do list an item at auction, I start it at the lowest price I would be happy selling it for in case only one person bids on it.

Because of their bulky size and heavyweight, we almost always ship signs via Parcel Post. I list these types of bulky items using calculated shipping so that the buyer pays the postage cost to their zip code. I make sure I have a shipping box for these signs before I list them, so I am not scrambling to find a box when they sell. My dad uses lots of bubble wrap and packing paper to secure these during transit. These signs are fragile, so you cannot be too careful when packaging them. The more packing materials you use, the better!

#8 BELT BUCKLES

Belt buckles can be highly sought after on Ebay if they represent a product, brand, or event. Plain old belt buckles are not going to cut it as far as reselling them online (unless they are made of an expensive material or have rare jewel or stone on them); there needs to be something special about them.

Living in Iowa, I am always finding John Deere belt buckles, although they are usually priced too high for me to make a profit on them. However, I have found other belt buckles that were promotional items for brands and products, including Lennox (as in the furnace makers), fishing tournaments, and fraternal organizations. I usually find belt buckles at estate sales; they are not produced as much these days as they once were, so finding them is always exciting as I do not often spot them.

Just as a coffee mug or plush toy will sell with a licensed brand on them, so will belt buckles. I would never have suspected a belt buckle from a Lennox dealer would sell on Ebay, but it did (and quickly). As with all items, before you list any belt buckle on Ebay, do a completed listing search to see if any like it have sold recently in order to determine a price. While most belt buckles sell in the $10-$25 range, there are some highly collectible pieces out there that can bring in hundreds if not thousands of dollars.

I only sell belt buckles at Fixed Price as there are rarely enough people to start a bidding war at auction. There is a "Vintage Belt Buckle" subcategory under the "Men's Clothing" category. Still, if I find a belt buckle that is branded with a company logo, I will often list it under the "Advertising" subcategory under "Collectibles."

I take two pictures of belt buckles for my Ebay listing: one of the front side of the buckle and one of the backside of the buckle. Unless I am positive of the metal, I will not specify what they are made of other than to just put "metal" in the description. While many belt buckles look like pewter, silver, gold, or bronze, most are basic metal with a finish coating on them.

Belt buckles are small and easy to ship, fitting into a bubble mailer. Some are very heavy, so be sure to get a weight before you list them if you plan to offer "free" shipping. If they are under 13-ounces, they can be shipped via First Class; over a pound, they will fit into a Priority Mail Flat Rate Bubble Mailer. So, the postage could range anywhere from $3 to $6; and if you are offering "free" shipping, you will want to build that cost into the selling price of the piece.

#9 BETTY BOOP

Retro characters are always popular, and Betty Boop is no exception. There is Betty Boop clothing and handbags, as well as figurines, Christmas ornaments, and jewelry. While most of the pieces I have come across are more modern, there are some vintage Betty Boop collectibles that sell for over $1000 on Ebay.

When looking at Betty Boop items at garage sales or thrift stores to resell on Ebay, you want to make sure the pieces you find have some age to them. Betty Boop merchandise has been mass-produced in recent years, even popping up at Walmart and Dollar Tree. If the label or marking reads "Made in China" with a recent year on it, you should likely pass. The exception to this is Betty Book clothing in larger sizes; plus size women's shirts featuring Betty Boop are hard to find new in the stores; so, if you spot them in good condition secondhand, they are worth picking up.

Ebay has an entire subcategory dedicated to Betty Boop (Collectibles – Animation Art & Characters – Animation Characters – Betty Boop), which shows you just how many items are out there on the resale market. As with any popular category, it is worth your time to study the completed Betty Boop listings to get an idea of what items sell, as well as which items do not.

#10 BETSEYVILLE BY BETSEY JOHNSON

Designer Betsey Johnson has been producing funky, high-end women's clothing and accessories for years. But she also has a more affordable line called Betseyville by Betsey Johnson, and it is these pieces that you are more likely to stumble upon at a garage sale or thrift store. I have found that Betseyville by Betsey Johnson pieces sell very nicely on Ebay, so I always keep my eye out for them.

I once went to a garage sale where they had racks of brand-new purses for sale for $30 each. However, in the back of the garage, they had one lone Betseyville by Betsey Johnson purse (brand new with tags!) for only $5. I snatched it up, and it sold within one day on Ebay for $59!

While I shy away from many designer label handbags due to the high-rate of forgery, Betseyville by Betsey Johnson is not a line that I have ever found counterfeited. These purses and wallets are easy to spot as they feature wild and colorful patterns with "Betseyville" printed on their fabric, inside label, zipper, and key fob.

We always make sure everything we sell on Ebay is in good, clean condition. Betseyville accessories usually have a shiny exterior material that is easy to wipe off. The condition issues I do come across with Betseyville are if the bag has studs on it; the finish on the points of these studs often wears off. While customers will still buy a Betseyville bag with some wear, you do want to make sure to disclose any condition issues in the listing.

To list handbags, I take a picture of the bag from all four sides as well as a picture of the bottom and a picture of the inside. When you list in the handbag category on Ebay (Clothing, Shoes & Accessories – Women's Handbags & Bags), Ebay provides item-specific fields within the listing for you to fill out. It is always in your best interest to not only fill out these sections (for the brand, color, and size) but also to put these details into the actual listing description.

Customers shopping for purses on Ebay want to know their measurements in length, width, and depth, as well as the strap drop (measuring from the top of the bag to the top of the strap handle). I also note all features such as zippers, snaps, and pouches. The more details you provide in your listing lessens the chance of having to deal with customer questions.

We keep large poly bags on hand for shipping purses; Betseyville bags, especially, are somewhat larger and bulky, making it hard to find a box for them. We wrap the bag up in bubble wrap and then surround it with packing paper to protect it inside of the bag during transit.

#11 BLOW MOLDS

We love to decorate for the holidays, and our basement is full of outdoor plastic lighted figures for Halloween and Christmas. You have likely seen these decorations, or you may even have them yourself. What you may not know, however, is that these are called "blow molds," and the vintage ones especially are very sought after on Ebay. However, even newer models will sell as they are getting harder and harder to find in stores.

While the plastic used to make blow molds tends to hold up well, the paint and finishing typically does not. It is rare to find these in absolutely perfect condition, and while some wear is expected, I pass up any with the paint more than 25% worn off.

Poloron, Union, Empire, Featherstone, and Beco are the brand names to look for on blow molds; they are molded right into the plastic on either the bottoms or backs of these pieces. Christmas carolers and reindeers are some of the most valuable designs. But it is not just Christmas blow molds that people buy; there are blow molds for Halloween, Easter, Thanksgiving, and even the 4th of July.

Buying these pieces to sell on Ebay does present a shipping challenge as the full-size figures are quite large. However, the vintage pieces tend to be small, table-top sized figures that are super easy to ship. I have picked these up in antique stores for $5 and sold them for as low as $20 and as much as $50.

While a blow mold without a bulb and/or electrical cord will sell, ones that include these will sell much better. You can pick these cords up at hardware stores for a few dollars. Selling blow molds WITH the electrical cord all ready to go is vital in getting top dollar. They will sell without a bulb and cord, but you will have to accept less.

Because even the smaller tabletop models are still larger than your average package, blow molds usually need to ship via Parcel Select. Be sure you have a box for shipping ready before you list a blow mold, so you are not scrambling to find one when it sells.

#12 BUDDY BEARS FROM BERLIN

If you have read any of my Ebay books or watch my Ebay videos on YouTube, then you already know that coffee mugs are some of my favorite items to pick up to resell on Ebay. People are constantly asking me what mugs sell well, and if you are one of those people, you can add Buddy Bears to the list!

Buddy Bears are teddy bears that started as a series of life-size fiberglass painted bear sculptures in Berlin, Germany. The first bears appeared on German streets in 2001. As with all popular attractions, the Buddy Bears soon made their way to merchandise, including mugs and teacups.

If you spot a coffee mug with a teddy bear on it, simply turn it upside down to see if it is marked as a Buddy Bear. If so, and if it is cheap, snatch it up for a quick flip of $10-15 on Ebay. In addition to coffee mugs, there are also Buddy Bear figurines, which can sell for upwards of $50 online.

Note that some other lines of teddy bears may be labeled as "Buddy," but you want to look for items explicitly marked as "Buddy Bear" and made in Germany. To list Buddy Bears on Ebay, be sure to put both "Berlin" and "German" in the title.

It is rare to find Buddy Bears here in the United States; most of the ones sold on Ebay come directly from Europe. Finding them here means someone actually picked them up overseas, likely during a vacation. So, while Buddy Bears merchandise is not at most garage sales and thrift stores, they are another item to add to your memory bank of things to look for while out picking.

#13 BREAD MAKERS

If you hit up a lot of garage and estate sales or frequently check the housewares section at your local thrift store, chances are you will come across bread makers. I myself bought a bread maker years ago (long before I sold on Ebay) with the intention of baking loaves of fresh, homemade bread. I made one loaf...and I then sold the machine at my own garage sale for $10. Most people do the same thing I did, which is why you can easily find bread makers secondhand.

There are high-end bread makers such as Zojirushi and Breville that can sell for hundreds of dollars on Ebay, depending on make and model. The newer the machine and the more bells and whistles it has, the more money it will sell for. More common brands you are likely to find secondhand are Braun, Panasonic, Oster, and Cuisinart.

In order for you to get top dollar for a used bread machine, you are going to have to ensure that it works. So, unless you have seen it in action first hand, be very careful stating the condition. If you find a bread maker cheap but do not want the hassle of testing it, you can simply break it down and sell it for parts.

Bread machine parts and accessories are easy to pull out and easy to ship, and there are lots of people looking for replacement pieces. The inside pan with kneading paddles, for instance, can go for as high as $50 alone if it is from a high-end brand such as Zojirushi; but even more common brands can sell for $25.

Most sellers do not want to test these machines nor take on shipping them as they are so heavy and bulky; hence, most people piece these out and sell the parts. If you do decide to sell a complete unit, note that it will likely have to ship via Parcel Post due to its weight and size. Be sure you have a plain cardboard box at the ready before you list a bread maker so you'll be prepared when it sells. And take care when packing it so that it does not break during transit by using lots of bubble wrap and packing paper or peanuts.

#14 CABELAS CLOTHING

Cabela's is a popular chain of mega sporting goods stores in the Midwest. Their stores are HUGE and appeal mainly to camping, fishing, and hunting enthusiasts. In addition to selling big-name national brands, they also have their own line of clothing. And Cabela's branded clothing is usually an easy sell on Ebay.

I have sold both men's and women's Cabela's clothes, everything from winter parkas to fishing shirts. As with all clothes, you want to make sure any Cabela's clothing you pick up is in good condition (after all, it was initially purchased by someone who likely wore it during rigorous outdoor activities). Larger sizes will sell faster than smaller ones. However, I have never had a Cabela's clothing item, regardless of size, not sell. So, if I spot a well-made Cabela's coat in size small for a dollar or two, I will pick it up.

In addition to shirts and jackets, Cabela's also makes leather hiking boots that can bring in upwards of $100 on Ebay. They also produce camping and fishing equipment. My general rule of thumb is that if an item is marked as Cabela's and priced low, I will pick it up.

I price Cabela's clothing on Ebay anywhere from $20 for shirts to up to $50 for larger-sized coats. We wash all clothing that we pick up secondhand before listing it on Ebay. When listing in the clothing categories, Ebay provides you with several item specific fields for things such as brand, material, color, and sizes. It is a good idea to not only fill these fields in but also to put the same information within the item's description field. Putting the specifics in both areas cuts down on customers messaging you with questions because they only looked at one section and not the other.

I provide three measurements for shirts and coats, all taken with the garment lying flat on a table: pit-to-pit (tape measure drawn from under one armpit across to the other); sleeve (tape measure drawn from the shoulder seam to the cuff; or from the collar to the cuff if there is no seam); and body length (tape measure drawn from the top of the shoulder to the bottom hem).

Cabela's shirts weighing under 13 ounces can easily be shipped in a poly mailer, while heavier pieces can be rolled up and shipped in a Priority Mail Flat Rate Bubble Mailer. For larger coats that cannot fit into an envelope, we use large poly bags. We wrap the coat up in packing paper before putting it in the shipping bag to provide an extra layer of protection during transit.

#15 CANDY MOLDS

More and more people are taking up baking, including candy making, so that that plastic candy molds can sell well on Ebay. I was able to pick up a whole box of Wilton candy molds for 25-cents each, and I sold them all to a lady in Germany for $40. Wilton is the leading brand for candy molds, but you may also find them from specialty shops such as William's Sonoma.

The more unique and detailed the candy mold, the better it will sell, although selling them all in a lot like I did is easier for both listing and shipping as opposed to selling them individually. Most people who buy candy molds want a bunch of them to add to their collections, so lots are the way to go.

Note that while you'll most likely find plastic candy molds while out picking, there are also vintage metal molds that you may be lucky enough to stumble upon. These molds can sell for upwards of $100 on Ebay; the most popular of these are molds were produced to make chocolate Easter bunnies and chickens.

In recent years, companies have started making silicone candy molds, which hold up much better than the plastic ones. They also cost more at retail than the plastic versions. The best sellers of the silicone molds are ones from licensed brands such as LEGO and of cartoon characters.

As I mentioned, I sold a large lot of candy molds to a buyer in Germany; so, it is crucial that you open up any molds you list on Ebay to international buyers. I ship internationally through Ebay's Global Shipping Program; the buyer pays the shipping cost for me to send the package to Ebay's shipping center, and Ebay then handles all customs forms.

Ebay also takes responsibility for any packages that are lost or damaged. If you have been nervous about shipping internationally or are wary of the Global Shipping Program, I urge you to give it a try as not only will it will increase the number of customers you can sell to, but it is also so much easier than trying to ship internationally directly from you to the customer.

#16 CARHARTT CLOTHING

Carhartt is a brand of clothing sold at Sears and agricultural retailers such as Farm & Fleet and Tractor Supply. Their heavy parkas, denim, and overalls are meant for those working outside, whether on farms or construction sites. The clothes are sturdy and well-made, and their retail price reflects their quality. So even though they sell at retail at lower-end department stores, they are still a good seller secondhand on Ebay.

I have sold both men's and women's Carhartt clothing, including casual button-front shirts, denim jackets, and winter coats. They also produce denim jeans and overalls, canvas work pants, vests, and sweatshirts. Their camouflage jackets are particularly valuable, bringing in a few hundred dollars on Ebay. While most people think of men's clothing when they think of Carhartt, I have sold women's Carhartt denim jackets for $30. However, most of the Carhartt clothing I come across is for men.

Because some Carhartt pieces are worth quite a bit, be sure to do a completed listing search on Ebay before listing anything to see what the going rate is. I always list clothing at Fixed Price as the chance of two people of the same size wanting the exact same item at the exact time it is at auction is rare.

When picking up Carhartt clothing to sell on Ebay, it is important to check for wear and tear; after all, these are working clothes, and whoever bought them originally bought them to WORK in. Carhartt clothing is washable, so if you find a piece that is a bit dirty, it should wash up fine.

To sell clothing successfully on Ebay, you will need to provide accurate measurements. For shirts and jackets, I lay the garment on a flat surface and take three measurements: pit-to-pit (tape measure drawn from under one armpit across to the other); sleeve (tape measure drawn from the shoulder seam to the cuff; or from the collar to the cuff if there is no seam); and body length (tape measure drawn from the top of the shoulder to the bottom hem). For pants, I measure the waist (tape measure drawn from one side of the waist to the other) and inseam (tape measure drawn from the crotch to the hem).

Carhartt clothing is usually made from heavier fabrics, so even the men's dress shirts can weigh over a pound; I usually ship them in a Priority Mail Flat Rate Bubble Mailer. The jackets and coats are too big to be rolled up into envelopes; however, so for bulky pieces, we use large poly bags. We wrap the coat up in packing paper before putting it in the shipping bag to provide an extra layer of protection during transit.

Because the clothing categories on Ebay are so competitive, it is best to list clothes with "free" shipping. However, shipping is never free as someone – the seller or the customer – has to pay for it. That's why it is important to have a digital scale so that you can weigh items before you list them in order to build the cost of shipping into the price of the item. To do this, I go to the USPS website and calculate the shipping from my zip code to a zip code in Hawaii, which is the furthest distance a customer could live from me. I then add that price into the asking price of the item.

#17 CATHOLIC MISSALS & PRAYER BOOKS

In the first volume of my "101 Items to Sell on Ebay" series, I talked about vintage Bibles and how well they sell on Ebay. A similar item is Catholic Missals, as well as any Catholic prayer book, which I can usually find for less than $1 at estate sales. And where there is one Catholic prayer book, there tend to be many; so often, I am able to buy several at one sale.

While these small books can sell on their own, twice now, I have sold lots of 12 books each for $100. One went to a Priest in Australia. Bibles, hymnals, and Catholic Missals, and prayer books sell well internationally, so be sure your listings are open to buyers worldwide. Ebay's Global Shipping program takes the work and stress out of shipping overseas, so there is no reason not to opt-in.

Most vintage Missals and prayer books I find are in relatively poor shape with loose spines and even missing pages. However, that does not prevent them from selling on Ebay. I make sure to take several pictures of these books (front cover, back cover, outside spine, all of the front pages, and a couple of pages of the main text) and to describe their condition as best I can. I measure books and include the number of pages they have in the listing. I also copy everything from the first page of the book (title, editor, publishing house). Vintage books sell best when they have a year inside; often, the year is printed on the title page's backside.

The poor condition of these books is another reason why I like to lot them together as I don't have to meticulously describe each one. When listing a lot of several books, I take one main picture of all the books together, several shots of groupings of book covers close up, and then a few shots of the books open to one page. I list the books included in the lot with their titles and dates, and I then describe the overall condition of the lot rather than each book individually.

I list vintage books in the "Antiquarian & Collectible" subcategory under the "Books" category. These books qualify to ship via Media Mail, although if I am selling a single book that weighs under 13 ounces, I will ship it via First Class as it is cheaper than Media and will arrive faster. We keep a wide variety of plain cardboard boxes on hand for shipping books Media Mail. We wrap books in a sheet of bubble wrap and then use packing paper in the box to protect it during transit.

I usually ship media products with "free" shipping, offering Media Mail for free but charging for the faster rates of Parcel Select or Priority Mail. I also charge shipping for international orders. I make sure that the cost of shipping gets built into the selling price. For example, if I have a book that I think will sell on its own for $9.99 with the buyer paying shipping and that the postage will cost $4, I will price the book at $14.99 with "free" shipping. Not only will I make a little extra money on the shipping this way (which goes towards purchasing packing materials), but buyers psychologically think they are getting a better deal with "free" shipping, even though they understand that the shipping cost is built into the price of the item.

#18 CATHY CARTOON COLLECTIBLES

I loved reading the comic strip "Cathy" when I was growing up. Written by cartoonist Cathy Guisewite, "Cathy" followed the life of a woman struggling with family, work, friends, dating, and dieting. The strip debuted on November 22, 1976, and it ended its run on October 3, 2010. The end of the series has created a stronger demand for "Cathy" collectibles, so be sure to pick them up when you see them if they are priced low enough.

In addition to books, "Cathy" coffee mugs and other novelties were produced during the series' run. However, very little merchandise was ever created for "Cathy," especially as compared to other cartoons such as "Peanuts" and "Garfield."

In excellent condition, the "Cathy" cartoon strip compilation books average around $10 on Ebay (a bit more for some titles). I have sold "Cathy" ceramic coffee mugs for $10, too. While these certainly are not big profits because "Cathy" items are so rare, I do enjoy picking them up to add to my Ebay store inventory. I usually find them for around a quarter at garage sales and estate sales, so I am willing to buy them and park them in my store for a while until the right buyer comes along.

The more time that passes since the end of the "Cathy" strip will only increase the value of these items. Because there is not a massive demand for "Cathy" merchandise, I only pick them up if they are in excellent condition and super cheap.

When listing anything "Cathy" on Ebay, make sure to put "Cathy," "Guisewite," and "Cartoon" into the listing title as there are lots of products (from clothes to make up") that is branded with the name "Cathy"; so you want to make it easy for customers to find your "Cathy" cartoon product. Most collectors will search for "Cathy Guisewite," so putting the full name in your title will help sell your item faster.

Because there is not a dedicated "Cathy" category on Ebay, I list "Cathy" products under the category of the specific item I am selling. For example, books go under the "Non-Fiction" subcategory under "Books; and mugs go under the "Animation Art & Characters" subcategory under "Collectibles."

#19 CHRISTIAN GIFTS

As I have discussed in both my first "101 Items to Sell on Ebay" book as well as this volume, Bibles, hymnals, and Catholic prayer books all sell well on Ebay. So, it is no surprise that religious items featuring Christian themes also sell. Hence, I am always on the lookout for faith-based products at estate sales that I can resell online.

When I was running my gift business, brand new Christian items such as journals and coffee mugs were some of my best sellers. However, even secondhand products, including Bible covers, crosses, Rosaries, and plaques, sell on Ebay.

As with anything you pick up to resell, the condition is important with Christian items; and a good brand name also helps. Because people are often buying these products to give as gifts, unless they are vintage, I only buy them in like-new, unused condition. Remember that stores like Dollar Tree sell a lot of cheap junk that features religious symbols, so always check the piece's bottom for a brand name and avoid items marked as "Made in China."

Journals, mugs, plaques, crosses, needlework kits, and décor featuring the Footprints poem or the Lord's Prayer may take a while to sell, but an Ebay buyer will usually come along. Gifts centered on Christian events such as baptisms are hard to find in stores, so they do well on Ebay, too. I once bought up a bunch of baptism gift products on clearance at a gift shop's going-out-of-business sale. All sold as soon as I listed them on Ebay for the price they had initially been sold for new.

#20 CIRQUE DU SOLEIL MERCHANDISE

If you have ever been lucky enough to catch a performance from Cirque du Soleil, you know what magnificent shows they put on! Through a combination of circus, gymnastics, dance, and music, each Cirque Du Soleil show is uniquely themed. I have been to the "La Nouba" performance at Walt Disney World in Orlando, Florida, twice, and I have caught a touring show here in Iowa. There are also several Cirque Du Soleil shows permanently based in Las Vegas.

Tickets for Cirque Du Soleil shows are pricey, as is the merchandise; so, if you find any tee-shirts, coffee mugs, programs, or other items secondhand for a good price, snatch them up to resell on Ebay. I recently stopped into the Cirque Du Soleil store at Disney World to pick up a magnet, and the smallest ones were a whopping $12. I have spent nearly $100 on very small items (magnets, a program, a small plush toy) between the three shows I have attended.

Cirque Du Soleil sells a wide variety of clothing and novelties branded for each show, and every piece has the official "Cirque Du Soleil" name on it. This is important to note as there are some shows that are called "Cirque" that are not actually affiliated with the "Cirque Du Soleil" brand. In addition to clothing and novelties, there are also Cirque Du Soleil DVDs and CDs.

As with any collectible you pick up to sell on Ebay, you want to make sure Cirque Du Soleil items are in excellent condition. Cirque Du Soleil shows tend to run for a long time, so many items you may see at garage sales are from shows that are still running. And in addition to Cirque Du Soleil selling their products at their shows, you can also buy them online. So, unless a product is from a retired show, it is not going to sell for as much as it did new. However, Cirque Du Soleil items usually sell for about 1/3 of their new retail price, which is a significant margin.

#21 CLIP-ON EARRING LOTS

While the stores are full of earrings for pierced ears, there are still many women out there who prefer the vintage look and feel of clip-on earrings. You can usually find piles of these at estate sales, and if you can get them cheap, be sure to pick them up as lots of vintage clip-on earrings do well on Ebay.

The bonus with selling a lot of clip-on earrings is that you do not have to sell each pair individually; simply lay them all out nicely, take some photos, and let the buyer have fun sorting through them. Make sure, however, to check that none are broken or missing stones. If you find broken or mismatched pairs, you can save them up to sell in a junk jewelry lot. I keep a box tucked away where I toss any broken jewelry I find; once it is full, I sell it as-is on Ebay.

However, while lots are easy to list and ship, if you find high-quality earrings with nice stones, you will get more money selling them individually. Be sure to check for a maker's mark and a metal marking on any jewelry you find. Vintage clip-on earrings from a high-end designer brand such as Chanel can sell for hundreds of dollars. And jewelry marked as gold or sterling are valuable just for the metal, not the design.

I recently lucked out and went to an estate sale where they were doing fill-a-bag-for-$5. I loaded my bag up with all of the clip-on earrings they had, took a few pictures, and quickly sold them for $30 with the buyer paying shipping. Because clip-on earrings are fragile and prone to breaking, be wary of shipping them in envelopes. We ship clip-on earrings in small cardboard boxes to ensure they are not smashed during transit.

#22 COLLEGE TEXTBOOKS

If you attended college or have put a child through school, I am sure you remember standing in line at the bookstore and handing over hundreds of dollars for textbooks. The secondhand textbook market is enormous, so always keep an eye out for these volumes at garage sales.

While most bookstores will repurchase textbooks for a fraction of the original cost, they do so only for a limited time. Therefore, students who were not able to get back to the bookstore during the buy-back window or who simply forgot to go end up with a pile of textbooks that are worthless to them after classes have ended. They often end up lugging these books back home after graduation, where their parents then try to sell them at a garage sale.

If you are lucky, you will find good condition textbooks that you can pick up for a couple of bucks to resell. It is not just new editions that sell, either; some medical books from several years back sell for over $100 on Ebay. Hardcover and softcover books both sell equally well. If you spot a textbook for a super low price, it is always worth the risk to buy it as it could very well sell for at least $20, if not more, on Ebay.

While textbooks are usually large and heavy, they do qualify for cheap Media Mail shipping. Be sure you have a plain cardboard box to ship them in so you will not be scrambling for a box when they sell. While most textbooks sell at the beginning of the school year and at the beginning of new semesters, you will want to list textbooks any time you find them as there is always going to be a student out there who needs a new copy immediately.

#23 COLUMBIA CLOTHING

If you frequent garage sales and thrift stores, you are well aware of how much-used clothing is on the secondhand market. Searching through the piles and racks of pants, shirts, and jackets can be overwhelming, which is why many pickers skip over clothes. However, there are some real gems to be found in the clothing sections; and one of them is the brand Columbia.

Columbia makes outdoor and sporty clothing for men and women, as well as coats for kids. Brand new, Columbia pieces are quite pricey. Therefore, it is only logical that they command a nice price on Ebay. I love finding Columbia jackets and parkas to resell, but I will also pick up men's shirts. All sell quickly and for a good profit. I typically find Columbia men's shirts for $2 that sell quickly for $20, and I have also picked up coats for $5 that sold for $50.

As with all clothing, the condition is key. Before buying a Columbia garment to resell on Ebay, be sure to look it over for rips and stains. Because the coats especially are so expensive, they seem only to get donated when they are damaged. I have found many Columbia jackets at Goodwill, but I have to put most of them back due to tears, stains, missing hoods, or broken zippers.

Larger size Columbia clothing sells best, although I have sold small women's coats. While I will likely pass on a small size men's Columbia shirt, I will get the smaller size jackets as the profit margin is much higher. Most Columbia clothing is labeled as either "Men," "Women," or "Child," which eliminates the need to try to figure out who the item was made for

To sell clothing successfully on Ebay, you will need to provide accurate measurements. For shirts and jackets, I lay the garment on a flat surface and take three measurements: pit-to-pit (tape measure drawn from under one armpit across to the other); sleeve (tape measure drawn from the shoulder seam to the cuff; or from the collar to the cuff if there is no seam); and body length (tape measure drawn from the top of the shoulder to the bottom hem).

While most Columbia men's shirts are lightweight enough to ship via First Class, the jackets and coats are too big even to be rolled up into a Priority Mail Flat Rate Bubble Mailer. So, for bulky pieces, we wrap them up in packing paper before putting them into a large poly envelope.

Because the clothing categories on Ebay are so competitive, I list clothes with "free" shipping. However, shipping is never free as someone – the seller or the customer – has to pay for it. That is why it is important to have a digital scale so that you can weigh items before you list them in order to build the cost of shipping into the price of the item.

#24 COOKIES ALL OVER COOKIE JAR

Secondhand cookie jars can be found at most garage sales, estate sales, and thrift stores. Since many people collect these, they can be great to resell on Ebay as long as they are in good condition. Check for a mark on the bottom of the piece and any chips or cracks. While I usually avoid anything marked as "Made in China," a cookie jar representing a cartoon character (such as Peanuts or Garfield) or brand (such as John Deere) would be an exception.

And while newer cookie jars will sell, there are some vintage cookie jars to definitely keep an eye out for as they sell very well on Ebay. One particular cookie jar you may come across is from Napco Pottery. It is an off-white jar with raised cookie designs all over. Dubbed the "Cookies All Over" cookie jar, it has a walnut on the lid and is, for lack of a better description, and, in my opinion, is downright ugly! However, it is highly collectible.

I actually have one of my own "Cookies All Over" jar that I inherited from a great aunt. And while it is not the prettiest thing to grace my home, it does have a certain vintage charm and sentimental value. While I would never sell my own jar, I have found others while out at estate sales that I was more than happy to sell on Ebay.

The last "Cookies All Over" jar I found that was in good condition cost me $4 during the half-off day at an estate sale. I quickly listed it on Ebay, where it sold for $59 with the buyer paying shipping. Do a Google search for this cookie jar and memorize what it looks like so you can pick it up if you ever see one. There are two different sizes, a medium and a large. Or just look for an ugly cookie jar with a tacky cookie design, and you will know you have found it!

To list any cookie jar on Ebay, we first wash it. I then take pictures of it from all four sides as well as of the bottom. I also take a photo of the inside and two pictures of the lid alone (one from the top and one from the bottom). Note that if you find a "Cookies All Over" jar with damage to either the canister or the lid, you can still sell the unbroken piece on Ebay as collectors of cookie jars are always looking to replace broken canisters or lids. Ceramic cookie jars are, of course, very fragile; therefore, you need to take care when shipping them by using lots of bubble wrap and packing paper or peanuts.

While some cookie jars may fit in the large 12x12x8-inch Priority Mail boxes, be sure to have plain cardboard boxes on hand just in case they are larger than the Priority Box. And they will need to go in plain boxes, anyway, to ship them out of the United States. Cookie jars are very popular with international buyers, so be sure to open up your listings to customers worldwide. Ebay's Global Shipping Program makes shipping to international buyers incredibly easy as well as risk-free.

#25 CRAFTOOL LEATHER TANDY STAMP SETS

Leatherwork is a craft still done by some artisans, and it's a trade more people are taking up these days. And while there are new sets you can purchase at craft stores or specialty retailers, vintage Craftool remains the gold standard, making them a hot seller on Ebay.

My only Craftool find and sale was a Craftool Leather Tandy Stamp set. These sets come in themes such as letters, numbers, holidays, and regions. I got a hold of three sets once that I was able to sell together for nearly $100. However, some sets sell for over $100 just on their own.

Even though these specialized pieces are not going to be at most garage sales you attend, I am still including them in this book to know them if you do see them. Most people at estate sales and thrift stores have no idea what these are; therefore, you may be able to buy them for a low price (unless the seller used them themselves and knows their value).

Note that in addition to stamp sets, there are many other Craftool leather working products such as tools, hand presses, and leather splitters that also sell for a lot of money on Ebay. The hand tools do incredibly well if you have a large lot of them.

Since it can be hard to recognize leather working products unless you yourself practice the craft, always look for the "Craftool" or "Tandy" mark. This is another "sold" category you will want to study on Ebay to familiarize yourself with what to look for when out picking.

#26 CRUISE LINE MERCHANDISE

It is my dream to someday take a cruise on the Disney Cruise Line, and I envy those who have taken cruise vacations. Cruising is quickly becoming one of the most popular vacations, with travelers developing loyalty to the various cruise lines.

All cruise lines have their own merchandise, most of which you can only get it on the actual ships. This makes cruise line merchandise and souvenirs great items to pick up for resale on Ebay as many people are looking to add to their collections or to replace lost or damaged items. Vintage cruising souvenirs are, of course, sought after by collectors, but even merchandise from modern ships can sell.

Whether it is a shirt or a coffee mug, a towel, or a bag, you can usually find cruise branded items for cheap at garage sales. Ensure the items are in good condition; that means no rips or stains on clothes and no cracks on ceramics or picture frames.

I have found Disney Cruise Line to be the most sought-after brand when it comes to Ebay. However, I have sold Royal Caribbean and Norwegian cruise line items, too. In addition to clothing, bags, and coffee mugs, look for pins and ship models. And always pick up anything vintage such as brochures or menus.

#27 DUNGEONS & DRAGONS

I have never played any role-playing games, so Dungeons & Dragons is a foreign concept to me. However, I do know to pick these products up when I see them secondhand as they are fantastic items to resell on Ebay!

The D&D games usually do not have too many pieces, so figuring out if a set is complete is pretty easy as all of the pieces are detailed on the outside of the boxes. These games have devout followers who tend to hold on to them for many years, so you might not find too many of these at garage sales, but still, keep your eyes peeled for them. I once sold a lot of just D&D manuals for $100!

In addition to board games and manuals, there are also Dungeons & Dragons miniature pieces, magazines, DVD's, and collectible coins. If you find smaller D&D pieces, I advise looking them up individually as some single items sell for hundreds of dollars on their own.

Dungeons & Dragons is an entire subcategory on Ebay under the "Toys & Hobbies" main category (Toys & Hobbies – Games – Role Playing Games – Dungeons & Dragons) with multiple subcategories to further narrow down the search for customers. If, like me, you are not family with D&D, take a little time to study the "sold" completed listings to get an idea of what to look for.

#28 1980'S BARBIE DOLLS

I am a child of the '80s, and I still have a pile of Barbie dolls from that era (Although I scalped all of my dolls, so they are all bald!). My favorites were Cowboy Barbie and the Barbie who kissed when you pushed a button on her back. Most collectors and resellers focus on the original Barbie dolls from the late '50s and early '60s (Barbie was introduced in 1959), and while those vintage dolls are very valuable, the 1980's dolls are also highly sought after.

I was once at an auction where a sad pile of Barbie dolls, just like the ones I have from my childhood, was not getting any bids. For fun, I ended up bidding and got them all for $3. I put them up for auction on Ebay and was shocked when a bidding war broke out! The winner was from Japan, and she paid $60 plus shipping for the lot.

Barbie dolls that still have their jewelry (earrings, rings) will command a higher price than those that do not. Having the original clothing is also important. And while vintage Barbie dolls that are still brand new in the box will, of course, always command the highest prices, do not overlook unboxed dolls or dolls in rough shape like the ones I sold.

In addition to the 1980's Barbie dolls, also look for 80's Dream House furniture and accessories such as the above-ground swimming pool (which I myself got for my 5th birthday) and the remote-control car. If you are unsure of the time frame of any Barbie dolls or accessories you are trying to sell on Ebay, you can list them as "vintage" and try selling them using an Ebay auction (which is what I did on the lot of dolls I bought at the auction house)

Bottom line: Just because a Barbie is not from the 1950s or 1960s does not mean she is not valuable!

#29 EMPTY PAPER TOWEL & TOILET PAPER ROLLS

Other than doing a bit of knitting and beading, I am not much of a crafter. However, crafting is HUGE these days, thanks in big part to the popular website Pinterest. I have sold many different crafting products on Ebay, such as stamps, scrapbook paper, yarn, and beads; so, I know that there is a big market for craft supplies. Even so, I was stunned when I found out that crafters were seeking empty paper towel and toilet paper rolls. Yes, you read that right: empty paper towel and toilet paper rolls will sell on Ebay!

Do a Google search of "toilet paper roll crafts" to see all of the creative ways people are using empty toilet paper rolls to make dolls, home décor, and even jewelry. Empty paper towel rolls are used to make everything from simple animal statues to complex dollhouses. While many of these projects are made by children in preschool classes, others are made by actual adult artists and designers. The wide range of items made from these cardboard rolls is amazing!

Because people want to get a large number of empty rolls at once, they turn to Ebay, looking for an entire lot. The going rate is $10 per 100 empty rolls. I realize that $10 is not a lot of money, but I look at it as FREE money as I would typically have just thrown these rolls away. You can also list them for $19.99 to $24.99 with "free" shipping as the postage cost can be anywhere from $10 to $15.

Keep a couple of plain cardboard boxes on hand to toss your empty (i.e., cleared off of all paper) rolls in. When you have 100 rolls, put them up at Fixed Price on Ebay. Ensure they are CLEAN and take pictures of them well organized (lined up neatly) in the shipping box to ensure a quick sale. Note that due to the size of the box, these will need to ship via Parcel Select. I do not use any additional packing materials when shipping these cardboard rolls; lining them up nicely in the box will keep them from rolling around during transit.

#30 ENESCO COLLECTIBLES

There are so many brand names of collectibles out there that it can be hard to know which ones are good for reselling on Ebay and which ones are duds. Most estate sales that I attend have table after table of ceramics, and I lift up every single one looking for good brand names. And while not all pieces under a specific brand will sell, Enesco is one name that seems to have more hits than misses.

Note that there are some Enesco lines, such as Precious Moments and Cherished Teddies, that are almost always NOT good sellers on Ebay. While there are some rare pieces in those collections that do have some value, as a general rule, I do not pick them up. Fortunately, however, there are plenty of other Enesco branded items that do sell well on Ebay and that are relatively easy to pick up cheap at garage sales, estate sales, and thrift stores.

Enesco has several licensed brands in its catalog, including Department 56, Disney, John Deere, and Snowbabies. These are typically the collections that do well on Ebay. The more bells and whistles an item has, the better it will sell. For example, a basic Department 56 Christmas village house may not bring in much money, but one that is co-branded with Coca-Cola and plays music will.

Another example is for Snowbabies. There are hundreds of Snowbabies on the secondhand market, but it is hard to find them for less than $5 at garage sales. Many only sell for $10 on Ebay; after taking out Ebay and PayPal fees, there is little room for profit unless you can pick them up for a dollar or less. The exception is a very old and rare Snowbaby or one that is co-branded with a licensed name such as Disney. As with any collectible, unless you know for sure that what you are buying has value, never pay more than a dollar or two.

Note that because the current Enesco lines are sold in stores such as Hallmark that it is the older, out-of-commission pieces you want to look for. Most Enesco pieces are dated, so always look for ones that are five years or older to ensure they are not still new in the marketplace. Having the original box is nice, but it is not always necessary for resale. Enesco pieces are clearly marked as such on the bottom, making them incredibly easy to identify.

As with all collectibles, condition counts. Most Enesco items are made of ceramic, so be sure to carefully examine all pieces for any chips or cracks. Take photos of all sides of the piece as well as of the bottom where the brand is stamped. When I am listing an Enesco piece on Ebay, I do a completed listing search to see what the current selling price is. I list almost all Enesco collectibles at Fixed Price as there is not enough demand to sell them at auction. Enesco collectibles may sit in my store for a while until the right buyer comes along. Still, I admire many Enesco products myself and like having them in my Ebay inventory mix.

#31 FAST FOOD MERCHANDISE

If you go to a lot of garage sales, you likely find bunches of McDonald's Happy Meal Toys. While the newer ones, even still new in package, are not worth much on Ebay, the vintage pieces still have value, although the market for them has cooled off in recent years. The toys from McDonald's and Burger King sell best when you have the entire set.

However, do not limit yourself to only looking for fast food toys to sell on Ebay as other branded items can actually sell even better. I have sold vintage Hardee's coffee mugs and McDonald's neckties on Ebay for a fast $10 each. Even a McDonald's uniform polo shirt is an easy $20 on Ebay. Ashtrays with the company logo on them are very sought after by collectors as they are no longer made as smoking is now banned inside of restaurants.

I am always looking for advertising pieces, and fast food items fall into that category. Novelties such as mugs and clothing were sometimes only offered to employees, meaning they are harder to find and more desirable to collectors. As with anything you are looking to resell, the rarer it is, the more money you will make.

One fast-food item you will likely come across quite frequently are the glasses that the restaurants either gave away or sold back in the 1970s and 1980s. In addition to glasses with the McDonald's characters on them, McDonald's, Burger King, A&W, Wendy's, and other chains all partnered with licensed brands such as Disney for various movie tie ins. These glasses do sell if you have the complete set; single glasses only bring in around $8 at most, oftentimes much less. However, the challenge then becomes shipping an entire set of glasses so that they do not break. If you do come across a set of these glasses, or if you decide to pick them up to save until you have the complete set, just keep in mind that you will need to package them to prevent breakage securely.

#32 FENTON

As I previously mentioned, nearly every estate sale I attend has table after table of china, pottery, and glass. Most of it is worthless junk, but I always pick up every piece to check the bottom for a maker's mark. One name I always look for is Fenton, which has been producing glassware since 1907. They are most famous for their carnival glass, but they also have produced a lot of pottery.

There is a lot of knock-off Fenton out there, so it is vital to make sure a piece is actually stamped as Fenton before buying it to resell on Ebay. Fenton is one of the brands that has seen a decline in value as more and more people are finding it to resell online, but there is still a nice profit to be made. Just be sure not to overpay; many people know the Fenton name and price it at full retail price at their garage and estate sales. It can be easy to get carried away and overpay in the excitement of finding a Fenton piece, but that leaves you little room to make an actual profit.

Condition on Fenton pieces is critical. In addition to checking for cracks and chips, note how much of the paint has faded. I have passed up a lot of Fenton in my time because of condition issues. I have seen Fenton cookie jars and teapots that were unfortunately worthless due to the paint fading over the years or because there were huge cracks on their lids.

In addition to smaller pieces such as tableware, there are also Fenton lamps and larger pieces of glass that can sell for hundreds if not thousands of dollars on Ebay. However, you are most likely going to find the tabletop items while out picking. As with any collectible brand, it is worth your time to study the completed Fenton listings on Ebay to learn what to look for. A recent search of "sold" Fenton pieces on Ebay brought up nearly 13,000 listings, so there are not only a lot of Fenton products available but also a large number of buyers!

#33 FIRE-KING GLASSWARE

Fire-King has been produced by Anchor Hocking since the 1940s. It is a brand of glassware that looks similar to Pyrex. There are all kinds of Fire-King items out there, including bowls, mugs, vases, pitchers, and dishes. All pieces are marked on the bottom as Fire-King Anchor Hocking, so they are very easy to verify as authentic. There are many knock-off Fire-King products out there, so always check for a mark before picking up anything to resell on Ebay.

My favorite Fire-King items to find for resale on Ebay are the milk-glass mugs, which are "milky white" cups. Finding these with licensed characters such as Disney or Peanuts is always exciting for me as they sell exceptionally quickly on Ebay. However, finding them in good condition is challenging as the designs tend to wear off over time. These pieces are not dishwasher safe for that reason, but still, people put them in their dishwashers and destroy the designs.

In addition to the white milk-glass mugs, Fire-King also produced various sets of colored milk glass dishes, the most popular being a line of green tableware called "Jadeite." A blue milk-glass variety called "Azurite" was also produced. These mid-century modern dishes are highly collectible, especially the full sets. Since shipping a full set of dishes is more risk than I personally like to take on, I always piece sets out.

Other pieces of Fire-King to be on the lookout for are their nesting mixing bowls (which are sometimes mistaken for Pyrex) and their white bowls for stand mixers. There are still many people who use their vintage stand mixers and who are looking for replacement bowls.

I rarely pass up any piece that is marked as Fire-King as long as it is in good condition with no chips, cracks, or fading of the prints. While most estate sales and thrift stores know to markup Pyrex, few know the value of Fire-King, meaning it is usually pretty cheap to pick up.

#34 FOOD NETWORK COOKBOOKS

Most estate sales I go to have at least one pile of cookbooks for sale. While many are duds in terms of them selling well on Ebay, there are some I look for, including those by the Food Network chefs. Ina Garten (The Barefoot Contessa), Ree Drummond (The Pioneer Woman), and Giada de Laurentiis are just a few celebrity chefs whose cookbooks sell well on Ebay.

Since these books are newer releases, not vintage, the condition is critical. While someone will pay top dollar for a vintage Betty Crocker cookbook in only fair condition, Food Network cookbooks need to be in excellent, like-new condition in order to sell. The books to look for are hardcover versions with the dust jackets. Avoid the softcover, paperback books as they are not as desirable.

In addition to the cookbooks, also look for Food Network magazine issues, which sell well in lots. The Food Network has already released DVD's, the most valuable of which are the ones featuring Alton Brown.

Note that there are many chef-branded cookware and dishware under the Food Network name that are sold at discount stores such as Kohls and Target. These pieces often get marked up secondhand because of their branding, but most have no more value than similar products under different brand names.

#35 FOSSIL WATCHES, CLOTHING & ACCESSORIES

Fossil is a brand of watches, clothing, and accessories. Because their watch bands and purses are made of genuine leather, they have a nice re-sale value on Ebay. Many thrift stores overlook this brand and stick the Fossil bags in with the cheaper purses; so, if you are lucky, you will be able to find these at a low price.

Fossil pieces are very clearly marked and not a brand that scammers knock-off, making picking them up a lot safer than, say, a Coach purse that could very well be a fake. The average selling price for a leather Fossil handbag on Ebay is $50, although rare prints can go for hundreds. As with anything you are listing on Ebay, be sure to do a completed listing search to determine the current going price. Fossil bags are very popular, making them one of the items you can take a chance selling at auction. Just be sure to start your auction at the lowest price you will be happy with, just in case only one bidder comes along.

The condition of Fossil accessories for resell on Ebay is very impor-tant, so be sure to look items over for rips or stains. Most Fossil bags are made of leather, but they do also produce some faux fabric and can-vas fabric items. While Fossil is known mainly for their watches and women's purses, they do also make some jewelry, men's shoes, wallets, sunglasses, and clothing. However, it is the watches and handbags that are best for selling on Ebay.

Ebay has a "Women's Handbags & Purses" subcategory under the "Clothing, Shoes & Accessories" main category. When I list a purse on

Ebay, I take pictures of it from all four sides as well as the bottom. I also take a photo of the inside. I fill out all of the item specifics within the listing (color, brand, measurements, material, country it was made it), and I also put that same information in the listing description. Putting the information into both sections will cut down on questions from customers who only look at one area.

To sell a handbag on Ebay, you will want to provide three primary measurements: the width, the length, and the height. You will also want to include the "strap drop," which is the measurement from the top of the bag to the handle's top. Be sure to note all details, such as whether the bag is a zipper or snap and all extra pouches or pockets.

While some handbags will fit into the Priority Mail boxes, we keep a wide variety of plain cardboard boxes and poly bags on hand for those that do not. While a purse is not going to break during shipment, you still want to wrap it well in some bubble wrap or packing paper to give it an added layer of protection during transit.

Since leather bags can be heavy, be careful about listing Fossil bags with "free" shipping. Some of these purses can weigh as much as three pounds, and shipping an item that heavy across the country can cost up to $15.

#36 FRANK LLOYD WRIGHT

Frank Lloyd Wright's architecture is admired worldwide, which is why items bearing his name are easy to resell on Ebay. Many of Wright's homes and buildings are museums that the public can tour, and with every museum is a gift shop. Therefore, you may find Wright coffee mugs and other souvenirs secondhand at garage sales and thrift stores.

There are several Frank Lloyd Wright homes within a few hours of where I live, so I have been fortunate enough to find these items occasionally. Do a Google search to see if there are museums near you, and you may have luck finding these collectibles, too. As with most tourist attractions, the Frank Lloyd Wright merchandise varies from clothing such as shirts and ties to housewares and coasters.

In addition to souvenirs, there are also LEGO Frank Lloyd Wright sets that can sell for nearly $300 on Ebay. When selling any used, opened game or model kit such as LEGO, it is vital to make sure all of the pieces are included. Therefore, you either need to assemble the piece yourself to prove all of the pieces are intact or sell "as is" for a lower price.

Finally, always look the books at sales and thrift stores for any Frank Lloyd Wright titles, including coffee table photo books. While the price for books has decreased dramatically in recent years as people turn to e-readers, some secondhand books do still sell on Ebay. Condition, age, and edition number all play a huge part in selling any book, including those about or by Frank Lloyd Wright, for top dollar.

#37 GENERAL'S DRAWING PENCIL KITS & SKETCHING SETS

Drawing and sketching items are expensive to buy new in the stores, so picking them up secondhand is always a smart move. One brand to look for is General's, which are vintage and very high-quality. I once hit up an estate sale in the home of a former auctioneer and was lucky enough to score some of these sets for only a couple of dollars. While to me, they just looked like a box of pencils, to buyers, they were treasures that they were willing to pay a nice amount of money for!

The General Pencil Company is headquartered in Jersey City, New Jersey, making them one of the few brands that are still made in the U.S.A. The company's roots date back to 1860. Some of their most well-known and popular products are their charcoal drawing pencils. They also make a wide range of color and sketching pencils, as well as pencil sharpeners and how-to-draw books.

While brand new, unsharpened pencils and those still in their original packaging bring top dollar, General's pencils that have been sharpened can still sell. If you attend estate sales or auctions, you will likely come across bundles or even boxes of old pencils and pens; if they are cheap, pick them up to go through them as there may be some gems inside, include vintage General's pencils.

#38 GERMAN BIBLES & PRAYER BOOKS

There is a lot of German heritage here in Iowa, so I have found many German Bibles and prayer books while out picking over the years. One might assume these books would bring in big money, but they actually only sell for between $10-15. Therefore, I always make sure not to pay more than $1-2 for them. However, since I do sell many English Bibles and hymnals, I like adding German ones into my Ebay inventory mix. Many old books now get thrown away, so I enjoy picking them up and finding them new homes.

I am fortunate to have a few friends who speak German, so whenever I get a German book, they always kindly translate the cover page for me. However, typing the title into a Google search should help you figure out exactly which book you have. The more information you can provide in your listing about anything you are selling, including German books, the better.

Note that many vintage German Bibles and prayer books were actually printed in the United States, not in Germany, which is one reason they do not sell for too much money. Vintage books of any kind, especially Bibles and hymnals that were printed in Europe, bring in a lot more money on Ebay.

When listing Bibles and prayer books on Ebay, I take a photo of the cover, a photo of the back, and a photo of the spine. I then take pictures of the first few pages of the book (where the title information is) as well as one or two pictures of the main inside pages. I measure the length and width of the book, and I also include the number of pages. You would be surprised at how many customers will message you asking for these details if you do not include them in the listing.

I list vintage German religious books in the "Antiquarian & Collectible" subcategory under the main "Books" category on Ebay, instead of in the "Non-Fiction" subcategory. This allows me not to have to be as specific when describing the book's condition as this category is for old books, which of course, are not crisp and clean the way a new book is.

These German books do qualify for Media Mail, but if they weigh under 13 ounces, I will ship them via First Class in a bubble mailer. Not only is First Class cheaper than Media Mail, but it is also much faster.

#39 GOLF GIFTS & NOVELTIES

Golf is a popular but expensive sport. Therefore, golf accessories such as designer balls, tee sets, towels, and golf club covers with novelty designs or licensed brands on them sell well on Ebay. Note that there are plenty of affordable new golf items on the market, so secondhand items must be unique in order to sell.

I have had good luck selling golf-themed gifts such as coffee mugs and picture frames. Most golfers are hard-to-shop-for men, so people are always looking for Christmas, birthday, and Father's Day gifts for the guys in their lives who golf. While novelties such as cups and ties will not bring in the big bucks, they are usually cheap to buy secondhand, which results in a nice profit margin. I have purchased many golf themed coffee mugs over the years for 25-cents that I sold on Ebay for $10.

If you are not afraid to ship large, bulky items, then reselling golf clubs can be a lucrative Ebay strategy. However, you need to know which brands are valuable and which to leave behind when you are out picking if you plan to make money selling golf clubs. Unless you yourself are an experienced golfer with a strong knowledge of all of the brands and products on the market, be careful about picking these items up to resell.

However, if you do not want the hassle of researching and shipping golf club sets, you can still pick up golf accessories such as towels and club covers with the logos of universities on them. Living in Iowa, I have purchased and resold lots of the University of Iowa branded golf items. There are also fun cartoon themed golf novelties from brands such as Disney that sell well on Ebay.

The bottom line is that you do not have to play golf or even know much about the sport of golf in order to make money selling golf items on Ebay!

#40 HOW THE GRINCH STOLE CHRISTMAS

The Dr. Seuss classic, "How the Grinch Stole Christmas," is incredibly popular; so, novelties such as clothing, toys, and collectibles are easy sellers on Ebay. I have sold everything from Grinch ties to Grinch plush toys. There are a lot of Hallmark Grinch collectible Keepsake Ornaments, and Kohl's has also released Grinch themed books and plush. Whether a vintage piece or a new release, I have never gone wrong with picking up the Grinch! His dog, Max, is also very popular, as is Cindy Lou Who.

While most collectors are after Grinch items from the original cartoon special, there are buyers for the Blu-Ray discs of the Jim Carrey live-action film. With the decline in DVD sales due to people switching to Blu-Ray, and because of the fact that you can get the DVD's super cheap at Walmart, Target, and on Amazon, you'll only want to pick up the Blu-Ray disks to sell on Ebay if you happen to come across them.

And while the Blu-Rays of the newer movie version will sell on Ebay, when it comes to other Grinch products, you will want to look for items from the original cartoon. As with any collectible, condition counts; so, look over items carefully before buying them to list on Ebay. Plush toys especially need to be clean and in like-new condition unless they are a vintage piece, in which case some wear is to be expected. The line of Kohl's Cares plush Grinch toys are especially popular but need to be in good condition in order to sell on Ebay.

Several companies still hold the license for the Grinch, and every Christmas, new novelty items roll out at the discount big box stores. When picking up Grinch products to resell on Ebay, you want to stick with those that are no longer being manufactured. Most Grinch collectibles are printed with a date, so steer clear of items from recent years and only pick up those that are five years or older (the exception being the Kohl's plush).

#41 HARLEY DAVIDSON CLOTHING & COLLECTIBLES

Harley Davidson is another go-to name when it comes to picking it up for resale on Ebay. Not only are Harley motorcycles expensive, but their clothing, collectibles, and novelties are, too. Because of their high-value new, picking them up for a good price secondhand to resell on Ebay is always a smart move.

Harley Davidson produces a huge line of merchandise, including clothing, toys, home décor, kitchenware, and gifts. They even make pet clothes! I have sold lots of Harley Davidson shirts over the years on Ebay. All Harley dealerships produce their own branded clothing, which many bikers collect them during road trips. I recently went to a garage sale where I found ten women's Harley Davidson tee shirts from dealerships across the county; I paid $1 each and will sell them for $20.

When it comes to Harley Davidson clothing, the size is not an issue as it is the Harley brand people are buying. So, while I usually would not pick up small size jackets to resell on Ebay, I will if they are Harley. However, as with all clothing, you want to make sure the garments are in good condition with no rips or stains. I recently picked up some Harley jeans that ended up being worn on the inseam and stained with oil.

Note that there are many generic motorcycle clothing and novelties on the market, but it is the Harley Davidson branded ones you are looking for to sell on Ebay. All Harley products are clearly marked as such; if you do not see the Harley Davidson name on a piece, pass it up. But if you do find Harley Davidson products for a reasonable price, and they are in good condition, grab them and get them listed on Ebay ASAP!

#42 INK CARTRIDGES

If you have a printer, you know how expensive ink cartridges are. However, because people are continually upgrading their printers, it is very common to find unused ink cartridges cheap at garage and estate sales as well as in the bins at thrift stores. While ink cartridges come with an expiration date, most will still sell even if that date has passed.

It is important only to buy ink cartridges that are still sealed. HP cartridges are the most popular to buy and resell. I never pay more than a couple of dollars for cartridges, and I can sell them for at least $10 and often times more on Ebay.

When listing ink cartridges on Ebay, always do a completed listing search for them first to see what the current selling price is. While many will only sell in the $10-20 range, there are ones that are much more valuable that command a lot more money. I sell ink cartridges at Fixed Price rather than at auction as they are not likely to attract multiple bidders. I take a photo of the package's front and back, and I always include the expiration date. As I said, most cartridges will still sell past their expiration date as long as they are new and sealed.

Since ink cartridges are lightweight, I ship them via First Class Mail in bubble mailers. For lower cost cartridges, I will list them with calculated shipping so that the buyer pays the postage cost to their zip code. However, if the cartridge is particularly valuable, I will add a few dollars into the price to sell it with "free" shipping.

#43 IRISH NOVELTIES

Folks with Irish ancestry are a proud bunch, and they eagerly snatch up anything referencing their heritage. I have sold many Irish coffee mugs in my years on Ebay. I can usually find mugs for a quarter at estate sales, which I am able to sell for $10 quickly. I have also sold Irish themed tee shirts, buttons, and neckties. And I often find pottery marked as "Made in Ireland" at estate sales, which were picked up during European vacations.

Since Irish themed items are relatively hard to find, they are highly sought after on Ebay, which usually means they sell fast. Be sure to check the clearance racks after Saint Patrick's Day to see if you can find items to resell. If you can find decorations super cheap, they may be worth picking up to resell the following year.

Note that Irish items sell all year long, not just around Saint Patrick's Day; although in the weeks leading up to the holiday, they do sell better. However, people are always looking for Irish themed gifts to give at Christmas and on birthdays, so list any that you pick up immediately as you never know when a customer will come along.

When picking up novelty items, the condition is critical. Since these are lower-priced products, they must be in excellent shape to sell on Ebay. Look over shirts for rips or stains, and make sure any ceramics or pottery is free of chips or cracks. I list Irish themed products at Fixed Price as they are not items that attract multiple bidders.

While selling Irish novelties on Ebay is not going to make you rich, they are a fun item to add to your Ebay inventory!

#44 J. CREW CLOTHING

J. Crew is another can't-go-wrong clothing brand when it comes to picking it up to sell on Ebay. J. Crew makes high-quality (i.e., high-priced) clothing for men, women, and children. In addition to stores at regular shopping malls, they also have shops at outlet centers and sell online. Therefore, it is likely that you will be able to find some J. Crew pieces while out thrifting no matter where you live.

I have sold J. Crew jackets and shirts for both men and women. Because they are expensive, I do not find too many secondhand; but I am always on the lookout for J. Crew tags. I do not worry too much about size with J. Crew items due to their popularity. I have found that smalls sell just as well as extra larges in this brand.

A basic button front men's J. Crew shirt is an easy $20 on Ebay, with their flannel shirts bringing in as much as $80. J. Crew wool women's coats can bring in as much as $200 depending on condition, style, and size. Most of the J. Crew pieces I find to resell average me about $30 each on Ebay.

As with all clothing you sell on Ebay, the condition is vital. Be sure to check garments for rips or stains. I take pictures of the clothing from the front and back, as well as an up-close shot of the collar/tag area. And I take photos of special details such as buttons and pockets.

To sell clothing successfully on Ebay, you will need to provide accurate measurements. For shirts and jackets, I lay the garment on a flat surface and take three measurements: pit-to-pit (tape measure drawn from under one armpit across to the other); sleeve (tape measure drawn from the shoulder seam to the cuff; or from the collar to the cuff if there is no seam); and body length (tape measure drawn from the top of the shoulder to the bottom hem).

J. Crew shirts that are lightweight enough to ship via First Class get sent in poly bags. The jackets and coats, however, are usually too big even to be rolled up into a Priority Mail Flat Rate Bubble Mailer. So, for bulky pieces, we wrap them up in packing paper before putting them into a large poly envelope.

Because the clothing categories on Ebay are so competitive, I list clothes with "free" shipping. However, shipping is never free as someone – the seller or the customer – has to pay for it. That is why it is important to have a digital scale so that you can weigh items before you list them in order to build the cost of shipping into the price of the item.

#45 JANET NOTTINGHAM MUGS

Animal themed items are popular collectibles, with some people decorating their entire kitchens around pigs or chickens! I have talked a lot about the fact that I love to buy and resell coffee mugs on Ebay; I am always looking for profitable brands and exciting designs. And at every estate sale and thrift store I go to, there are often coffee mugs with various animals printed on them. While many are just dollar store pieces that are not worth anything on Ebay, one brand to look for is Janet Nottingham.

Janet Nottingham has designed coffee mugs with pigs, cats, and elephants on them. Made in England, these cute ceramic novelty mugs feature cartoon illustrations of animals and are relatively easy to resell online as there are not too many of them on the secondhand market. There are also ceramic trivets with the same animal designs on them, although thus far, I have only ever seen the mugs.

Most of these mugs were made in the late 1970s, which means they are vintage, making them even more appealing to collectors. The average selling price of these mugs is $10, although some can go for a bit more. So, while these are not a big moneymaker, coffee mugs, including these, are often only priced at a quarter, giving you a nice profit margin.

As with any ceramic, make sure there are no chips or cracks. I have had to pass up a few of these mugs in my time because they were damaged; they are older and fragile, making them prone to condition issues.

To list coffee mugs on Ebay, I take photos of all four sides as well as of the bottom and inside. I also list how tall they are in inches along with the mouth width. While you may assume all mugs are relatively the same size, buyers often want to know the exact measurements. So, providing these details in your listings will cut down on customer questions.

I list coffee mugs at Fixed Price on Ebay with the buyer paying shipping. Most mugs weigh between one and two pounds when boxed for shipment, so postage could be as much as $12 depending on how far away the buyer lives from you. As these mugs are incredibly fragile, take great care when packaging them by wrapping them in bubble wrap and surrounding them with lots of packing paper or peanuts. Most coffee mugs fit perfectly in the 7x7x6 Priority Mail box, and if you are buying and printing your shipping labels on Ebay, the shipping discount usually makes Priority cheaper than Parcel.

While selling coffee mugs such as these from Janet Nottingham will not make you rich, they are easy to find, cheap to buy, fast to list, and quick to package. Some days when nothing else seems to be selling on Ebay, it's the good 'ole coffee mugs that bring in the money!

#46 JIGSAW PUZZLES

There are a ton of jigsaw puzzles at garage sales and thrift stores, but only certain ones have resale value on Ebay. Look for puzzles from licensed brands such as Disney and Coca-Cola, which tend to do well on Ebay. Also, the more pieces a puzzle has, the better. Puzzles over 2,000 pieces are almost always a sure thing regardless of the design, but usually, most puzzles over 1,000 pieces will do well. Since jigsaw puzzles are available to purchase at nearly every discount store, puzzles on Ebay need to be unique in order to sell.

The key to selling secondhand jigsaw puzzles is guaranteeing that all of the pieces are included. Finding new, sealed puzzles are, of course, the easiest way to do this, but just because a puzzle is not new does not mean it will not sell. If you enjoy putting puzzles together, the best practice is to assemble a puzzle yourself to ensure all pieces are intact before listing it. However, if that is not something you want to do, just stick to new, sealed puzzles. You will be amazed at how many new puzzles you will find when out picking.

When I list a jigsaw puzzle on Ebay, I take a picture of the box's front, the back of the box, and if the box is open, a picture of the pieces. For sealed boxes, I obviously only take the first two pictures. I then copy the details on the box into the description (brand, country of manufacture, name of the design, number of pieces, age, the finished size of the puzzle). Ebay also includes these fields in the listing specifics, so you'd be wise to fill out the fields AND put the same information into the listing description as many customers don't look at the item specific fields (yet use them for searching) and will message you with questions.

Since puzzles are big, bulky, and usually over two pounds, I list them using calculated shipping, with the buyer paying the postage cost to their location. Rarely do jigsaw puzzles fit in the Priority Mail boxes, so be sure you have a plain cardboard box on hand to ship the puzzle you are selling.

#47 JOURNALS & DIARIES

Back when I was selling new gift items on Ebay and Amazon, one of my biggest categories was journals. Whether they were blank books with fun covers or guided diaries with prompts for writing, for years, I sold journals successfully online. And because quality journals are expensive (take a look around the stationery section at Barnes & Noble to get an idea of how much these cost), I still look for journals when I am out picking.

When looking for journals to resell on Ebay, I look for unused ones, well made, have a good brand name (after all, even Dollar Tree sells diaries), and have lots of lined pages. Themed journals, such as those for travel or pregnancy, do incredibly well as long as they are new, so be sure to check for any writing inside.

In addition to new styles of journals, also look for vintage ones. Often these can be found at estate sales, and in the case of vintage journals, it is perfectly fine if they are used. In fact, some buyers are actually looking for journals that were written in years ago.

In the same vein as vintage journals are vintage wedding scrapbooks, baby books, address books, and Christmas card list books. Unlike vintage journals that will sell if written in, you want to make sure wedding, baby, address, and Christmas books are unused. Often buyers are looking to replace a beloved worn-out book, so finding these blank can be challenging; if you do, snatch them up.

While journals are not going to make you a considerable amount of money, they are an excellent item to add in to your Ebay inventory. Be aware when listing them that not all will qualify for Media Mail. If the books are blank and/or spiral-bound, they will have to ship via standard post. If they are under 13-ounces when inside of a bubble envelope mailer, you can ship them via First Class. Journals with guided prompts in them do qualify for Media Mail, although if they, too, are less than 13 ounces, it is actually cheaper (and faster) to ship them via First Class.

#48 JUNK JEWELRY LOTS

Secondhand jewelry is everywhere; from garage sales and estate sales to thrift stores, you can find rings, bracelets, necklaces, broaches, and earrings in every shape, color, and style. There are a lot of pickers out there who scour through any jewelry they spot to see if any of it is stamped as gold or sterling silver. They are also looking for vintage pieces to sell on their own on Ebay or Etsy.

And while there is valuable vintage jewelry to be found, there is also a lot of junk on the secondhand market. In addition to a lot of jewelry having no resale value (most women's stores, as well as discounters such as Walmart and Dollar Tree, carry cheaply made jewelry), even pieces that may have once been desirable are often damaged and broken beyond repair.

However, do not dismiss broken jewelry, especially if it is cheap to buy, as damaged costume jewelry can well in lots on Ebay to crafters who are looking for junk jewelry to use in various projects. I have seen broken jewelry pieces used to cover jewelry boxes and picture frames, and some artisans even use broken pieces to craft new jewelry products.

Often times, you will find cheap bags or jars of broken and mismatched jewelry pieces at garage sales or on the shelves at thrift stores. Do not hesitate to grab these and save them up for a lot to list Ebay IF they are metal. Plastic beads are a dime a dozen and have no value on Ebay; if you pick a bag of plastic bead necklaces, put it back down. What you are looking for are metal parts from earrings, necklaces, and other jewelry pieces. And when it comes to junk jewelry, I have learned that the tacky and gaudy pieces are actually the most popular. While a pile of plain silver tone broken chains will not sell for much if at all on Ebay, a collection of big broken broaches with lots of stones and faux jewels will.

I often go to fill-a-bag estate sales and am able to buy up an entire table of miscellaneous jewelry for as little as $5. I have a designated Priority Mail Flat Rate Box to hold any junk jewelry I find. When it is almost full, I take one picture of it all in the box and then list it for a Buy It Now price with "free shipping (i.e., the shipping added in). I do not take detailed photos of each piece as the fun buyers have with junk lots is sorting through them looking for treasures.

To ship these boxes of jewelry, we just put all of the pieces into a big plastic bag and then use some packing paper to buffer the bag inside of the shipping box. Because the jewelry is already broken, there is no need to wrap each item individually.

#49 KEYBOARDS

I had two electric piano keyboards as a teenager, a Casio and a Yamaha. If you have ever looked at these new in the stores, you know how pricey they can be, which is why they do extremely well on Ebay. Some models can fetch thousands of dollars, but most secondhand keyboards from the 1980's and 1990's average around $100 on Ebay. Considering you can sometimes find these for as little as $5, that is an excellent return on your investment!

Finding older keyboards in good condition is the biggest challenge when it comes to picking these up to resell. I have had to pass up many keyboards over the years because the condition was terrible from being dropped or left out in the elements. Even a keyboard that looks relatively good on the outside may still have technical issues that prevent it from playing.

Always check the back of any keyboard you are considering picking up to resell on Ebay to ensure it is intact and that the battery compartment is not eroded. These machines always came with electrical cords, so be sure they are included. While replacement cords can be purchased, they can be expensive and hard to find. I will not buy a keyboard unless it is in excellent shape, in working condition, and has the cords.

If you have a smartphone with the Ebay App downloaded, be sure to do a completed listing search on any keyboards you come across to see what they are selling for online. The price range for these keyboards varies wildly depending on brand, size, features, and condition, so being able to look up the make and model quickly on your phone will help you from overspending or from potentially passing up a rare, valuable model.

Since the large keyboards are difficult to ship, I mainly look for smaller, tabletop models that I can buy for under $5 and easily flip for at least $25. If you do decide to list a large keyboard on Ebay, be sure you have a plan for how to ship it when it sells. The large keyboards are too big to be shipped Priority, and some are even too large to be shipped Parcel Select. Therefore, you will need to look into shipping via USP or FedEx, both of which are much more expensive than the USPS shipping services. Needless to say, you will want to use calculated shipping when selling keyboards on Ebay so that the buyer pays the postage cost to their zip code.

#50 KITCHEN-AID

If you have a Kitchen-Aid stand mixer or any other Kitchen-Aid products in your home, you know how expensive they are. That is why Kitchen-Aid items and accessories are always great to pick up for resale on Ebay. You can sell both the various appliances intact or piece them out for parts. In fact, most sellers prefer breaking down these large, heavy machines and just selling the replacement parts.

Shipping any small appliance is often tricky due to their size and weight, and many times the shipping cost is more than the item is worth. And because the appliances themselves can be purchased new for a reasonable price during a store sale (you can often get new Kitchen-Aid mixers at cost on Black Friday), a smart move is to only focus on selling replacement parts, which are easy to list and easy to ship.

Even though Kitchen-Aid stand mixers may be too large and heavy for you to bother with, they have many accessories that you might be lucky enough to find that are small and easy to ship. The bowls, paddles, and various attachments all sell well on their own. In fact, the time and hassle you will save listing and shipping individual pieces versus the entire model will often put you out ahead in terms of net profit.

In addition to the stand mixers, Kitchen-Aid also makes a wide variety of electric kitchen products such as food processors, ice cream makers, and toaster ovens. Note that the smaller tools such as hand mixers are not big sellers on Ebay, but their replacement paddles are. Again, think of these large items in terms of the parts you can pull them out, such as racks for toaster ovens or canisters for ice cream makers.

Kitchen-Aid items do not have to be electric to resell on Ebay, though. I once bought a mandolin on clearance at Sam's Club for $20, but I never used it. I decided to put it on Ebay, where it quickly sold for $40!

#51 LARAMI SUPER SOAKERS

As a kid growing up in the 1990s, I had several Larami Super Soaker water guns. Boy, do I wish I had kept them as some models can sell for upwards of several hundred dollars on Ebay! However, the average selling price is around $50, depending on the make, model, and condition. For a toy, you can often find for a dollar at garage sales, which is a significant profit margin!

Finding these guns at garage sales is always exciting, but you do need to be careful as there are a lot of look-alike Super Soakers, some with very similar names. I recently spotted a "Super Soaker" water gun that was brand new in its box and complete with the original $5 price sticker from Dollar General. When it comes to buying water guns to resell on Ebay, it is the Larami brand you want to look for. All Larami Super Soakers have "Larami" marked on them right in the plastic, usually on the gun's underside.

In order to get top dollar for these older water guns, they need to be in excellent condition and with all of their parts. Be sure to check the areas around the handles and where the water comes out of to make sure everything is in-tact, and always test them. If you have a gun in poor shape, you can still get a few bucks for it by selling it for parts.

Note that Super Soaker collectors are incredibly picky about condition. Even a gun that seems to work fine may have a small rubber piece missing, and you can rest assured that the die-hard collectors WILL complain and demand a refund if these guns are not 100% in-tact (unless you have disclosed otherwise). Listing these water guns "as is" can save you the worry of buyers complaining.

Some of these Super Soaker guns are very large and bulky, making shipping difficult. Most will need to be shipped via Parcel Select in a plain cardboard box. There are Super Soaker collectors worldwide (I myself have sold them to Japanese customers), so be sure to open up your listings to international buyers. Shipping through Ebay's Global Shipping Program makes sending anything internationally a breeze as Ebay assumes all risk for the package.

#52 LEGOS

Whether you played with them yourself as a child or have kiddos who currently love them, LEGOS are still one of the most popular toys out there. The little plastic bricks also cost a ridiculous amount of money new, which is why they have a high resale value on Ebay.

If you hit up enough garage sales, you will likely see buckets and bags of LEGOS. If they are priced right, definitely pick them up. The going rate for plain, basic LEGO bricks on Ebay is $8 per pound. Unique sets and mini-figures based on video games, TV shows, and movies (for example, Harry Potter or Star Wars) command a much higher price. When reselling LEGO sets on Ebay, you do need to make sure they are intact. Since I have no desire to assemble LEGO sets, I just lump all pieces in a lot and sell them "as is."

As I mentioned, the little mini figure people that come with some sets can sell for quite a bit on their own, more if you sell several together them in a lot. Just as the Harry Potter and Star Wars LEGO sets are valuable, so are the mini-figures that come with them. Some sets of just these figures can sell well over $100.

Before you buy LEGOS to resell on Ebay, make sure they are actually LEGOS and not a cheap knock-off. You can find a small LEGO logo on genuine LEGO pieces. LEGO pieces are small, and the logos on them are even smaller, but the logo is always somewhere on the piece.

The great thing about selling a pile of LEGOS is that you can just take one photo of the entire pile and then list them with the total weight. To ship LEGOS, we put them into a large plastic bag (or multiple bags if we have numerous pieces) and then use a bit of packing paper to buffer the bags from the shipping box. LEGOS are easy to list and easy to ship!

#53 LEVI'S

Garage sales and thrift stores are all overflowing with denim, but one brand you can always count on for good resale value on Ebay is Levi's. Men's Levi's 505 jeans are super popular worldwide, so if you do pick up Levi's to resell, be sure to open up your listings to international buyers. As I have mentioned several times already, Ebay's Global Shipping Program makes shipping to customers outside of the United States easy and risk-free.

Even better than current Levi's are vintage jeans, which are identifiable on the tag as the "E" is a capital letter instead of the small case letter you find on today's labels. Because of the value in vintage Levi's jeans, there are now, unfortunately, people who are producing knock-offs, so be sure to educate yourself about what to look for.

In addition to the "E," vintage Levi's jeans will have a single-digit stamped onto the buttons, a flat silver rivet with L.S.&CO-SF, a care tag if produced AFTER the 1970s, and a care tag that reads "Shrinks about 10%" if produced between 1970 and 1985. However, even newer styles of Levi's jeans can resell, especially if they are larger sizes.

It is not just Levi's pants that sell but also their denim jackets. I pick these up all the time for a few dollars at garage sales and thrift stores and depending on the size, style, and condition, I have sold them for as low as $25 and as much as $100. Also, look for Levi's jeans that are in colors other than blue, such as red or green. The jackets also come in various colors and are good sellers.

As I always say, when it comes to selling clothing on Ebay, the condition of the pieces is essential. Be sure to check garments for rips or stains.

I take pictures of the clothing from the front and back, as well as an up-close shot of the collar/tag area on shirts or the waist/label area on pants. I also take photos of special details such as buttons and pockets.

To sell clothing successfully on Ebay, you will need to provide accurate measurements. For shirts and jackets, I lay the garment on a flat surface and take three measurements: pit-to-pit (tape measure drawn from under one armpit across to the other); sleeve (tape measure drawn from the shoulder seam to the cuff; or from the collar to the cuff if there is no seam); and body length (tape measure drawn from the top of the shoulder to the bottom hem). For pants such as jeans, I measure the waist (tape measure drawn from one side to the other) and the inseam.

Levi denim products weigh over one pound when packaged, so you will need to ship these by Parcel Select or Priority Mail. If shipping via Priority, you can use the free Priority Mail boxes from the Post office, although you may be able to roll up some pieces and fit them into the Flat Rate Priority Bubble Mailers. If shipping Parcel Select, you can keep the weight of the package down by in plain poly mailer bags.

#54 LILLY PULITZER

Lilly Pulitzer is a designer brand of women's and children's clothing featuring bright, colorful patterns. If you live in a city where Lilly Pulitzer is sold, you might be lucky enough to find them secondhand at thrift stores and garage sales. Some pieces can sell for hundreds of dollars on Ebay, so be sure to do a completed listing search to see what your item is currently selling for. In general, Lilly Pulitzer clothing averages $50 on Ebay.

In my area, Lilly Pulitzer is neither sold nor worn. However, I have occasionally stumbled upon accessories, such as a small make-up bag that was a gift-with-purchase item with a perfume. It was actually hanging on the fence at a garage sale; I paid $1 for it and sold it quickly on Ebay for $10. As with any expensive designer brand, even the small accessories can bring in a nice little profit.

In 2015, Lilly Pulitzer partnered with Target to release a limited-edition line of clothing, accessories, and housewares. Many stores were mobbed with women grabbing entire racks of dresses, and almost immediately, these pieces were listed on Ebay. Few ended up selling for more than the retail price, and today they are selling for less. However, they do still sell; and these pieces are already showing up at garage sales and thrift stores.

Lilly Pulitzer is famous for their dresses and blouses, but they also make pants, skirts, sweaters, and swimsuits. In addition to clothing, they also produce cell phone cases, purses, wallets, jewelry, watches, home décor, and even pet accessories.

Be sure to examine Lilly Pulitzer pieces thoroughly for any rips or stains. We wash all clothing before listing it on Ebay, and I also include several photographs as well as measurements. While I always list clothing at Fixed Price, Lilly Pulitzer accessories such as bags and home décor at the types of items that can do well at auction since they are not size specific.

If you haven't sold clothing on Ebay before, one tip when starting out is to stick to the standard sizes such as Small, Medium, Large, Extra Large, etc., rather than fitted garments such as size eight or size 12. While a Large size shirt can usually fit several different people, specific sizes are much more restrictive. I have much better luck selling generally sized clothing than I do things that are fitted. And while you still want to provide measurements, whether the size is general or fitted, fitted clothing will often require you to take additional measurements. For faster, easier sales, I recommend sticking to the standard sizes!

#55 L.L. BEAN

There are only a handful of clothing brands that I don't ever hesitate to pick up, and L.L. Bean is one of them. The L.L. Bean company was started back in 1912, and to this day, they continue to manufacture clothing and accessories in Maine. Their high-quality clothing and outdoor recreation items are relatively expensive new, so there is a definite demand for them secondhand on Ebay.

Even if you do not have an L.L. Bean store in your area, note that they maintain a popular catalog and website; so, you still may find men's, women's, and even children's clothing from them in your area at your local thrift stores. They also have stores in outlet malls across the country, so their pieces tend to pop up secondhand nearly everywhere these days. The closest L.L. Bean retail store to me is about three hours away, but I still come across their items occasionally while out picking.

In addition to clothing such as shirts, coats, jackets, and vests, L.L. Bean also produces canvas tote bags. Customers can choose to have these bags monogrammed, but even a monogrammed L.L. Bean bag (often called a "Boat & Tote) can still sell on Ebay. I simply list any monogrammed bags in my Ebay store at Fixed Price and wait for a buyer with those initials to come along.

Other L.L. Bean products to look for are men's leather boots as well as luggage. Be sure to examine any items for rips or stains; while L.L. Bean is a good brand name, damaged pieces are not going to sell. To list L.L. Bean items on Ebay, I do a "sold" completed listing search to determine a fair price. I then list my item at Fixed Price. While I usually build the cost of shipping into the price of clothing in order to offer "free"

shipping, for heavier items such as shoes and luggage, I list with Calculated Shipping so that the buyer pays the postage cost to their specific
zip code.

As I have already discussed, I take at least three photos of shirts and
coats (front, back, and an up-close shot of the tag/collar); and I provide three measurements (pit-to-pit, sleeve length, and body length). For
L.L. Bean garments with lots of extra details such as hoods, belts, and
pockets, I take additional photos of those areas of the piece, and I also
list those extras in the listing. Providing as much detail as possible in
your Ebay listing will drastically cut down on customer questions.

#56 LOONEY TUNES COLLECTIBLES

I talk a lot about picking up Disney items to resell on Ebay, but another cartoon favorite I always grab is Looney Tunes. Whether it is Bugs Bunny, Daffy Duck, or the Tasmanian Devil, Looney Tunes merchandise can do very well on the secondhand market.

I find a lot of Looney Tunes men's neckties and coffee mugs while out picking. The Goodwill stores in my area all have racks dedicated to ties, and it is rare that I do not find at least one that is Looney Tunes. Warner Brothers holds the license for Looney Tunes products, so be sure the tag reads both "Warner Brothers" and "Looney Tunes" to ensure it is a legitimately licensed product.

Most of my small Looney Tunes finds go for around $10, so I never pay more than a dollar for anything. While they do not bring in much money, the Looney Tunes brand name does often bring customers to my Ebay store. So even if they do not buy the Looney Tunes item, they may buy something else. I look at most licensed brands in this way, as a way to draw traffic into my store. A Looney Tunes mug may not sell quickly, but it usually works to attract buyers to my other listings; so, for me, they are actually a form of marketing.

The rarer the Looney Tunes character, the more money it will sell for on Ebay. Yosemite Sam, for instance, is a lot harder to find than Bugs Bunny; and therefore, he usually sells for more. A "sold" completed listing search will give you an idea of how to price your item. Most Looney Tunes products do not ignite bidding wars, so I always list them at Fixed Price with Calculated Shipping so that the buyer pays the postage cost to their zip code.

Since Looney Tunes products do not tend to bring in the big bucks, I only pick them up if they are in excellent condition. That means no chips, cracks, or spoon marks on coffee mugs; and no rips or stains on ties. I have had to pass up a lot of Looney Tunes ties over the years due to damage such as giant stains on the front of them.

While most Looney Tunes items I find are newer pieces, I always pick up anything vintage Looney Tunes, such as comic books, figurines, or toys. Both Pepsi and Coca-Cola released Looney Tunes collectible glasses in the 1970s in conjunction with fast-food restaurants. Full sets of these can sell for upwards of $200. While these types of promotional glasses tend to not sell well on their own, some of the rare Looney Tunes characters such as Wile E. Coyote and Slow Poke Rodriguez can fetch $40 individually. Looney Tunes is one of the few brands of these collectible fast food glasses that I will pick up.

#57 MAKE-UP

You might be surprised to find out that make-up, everything from drugstore brands to designer lines, can sell well on Ebay. Whether it is due to a color being discontinued or because a particular brand is not sold everywhere, make-up that is new, unopened, and/or sealed is something to look for at both garage sales and on the clearance racks at stores.

Recently Dollar Tree had a considerable stock of Physicians Formula blushes and bronzers. These sell for upwards of $15 at full retail price, so savvy resellers snatched them up to sell on both Ebay and Amazon. I have re-sold make-up that I had gotten at estate sales or had received myself as a gift-with-purchase. Gift with purchase (GWP) make-up is a common find at sales because most women do not like all of the colors or products that came in the free gift set.

Again, make-up needs to be unused in order to sell it on Ebay. Listing it as even barely used will result in your listing being pulled. Most cosmetic products come with some sort of seal on them nowadays; a seal not only indicates the product is unused but that it is newer. Make-up, especially once opened, does expire after a time.

High-end brands that sell well on Ebay include MAC, Chanel, and Marc Jacobs. Because different make-up brands and colors are not sold in every country, be sure to open up any make-up listings to international buyers. Ebay's Global Shipping Program makes shipping outside of the United States incredibly easy as Ebay handles all of the customs forms and assumes all of the responsibility for the package arriving safely.

The only way around selling make-up that is not new is if the product is vintage. In the case of make-up from the 1940s or 1950s, you want to focus on selling the packaging, which will likely come with some product still inside. So, if you find a vintage compact of face powder, list the COMPACT, not the make-up itself.

Large lots of new make-up can sell for up to thousands of dollars on Ebay, usually to people who will break them down into smaller lots to resell. Be very careful about purchasing these lots as some will show a large photo of hundreds of packages, but the listing is actually just for a few pieces. If you find a lot you want to purchase, be sure to check the seller's feedback and to read the listing very carefully so that you know exactly what you are buying.

Make-up that is liquid or that contains alcohol cannot ship via Priority Mail or First-Class Mail; it will need to be shipped via Parcel Post. This includes liquid foundation and eyeliner, nail polish, and fragrances. If you are shipping make-up during the summer or to a warmer climate, take precautions to prevent melting by using thermal shipping envelopes.

#58 MAKE-YOUR-OWN COOKBOOK KITS

When I sold new gift items on Ebay and Amazon, one of my top sellers were cookbook kits, which were binders filled with blank pages and accessories such as pockets and blank recipe cards to create a personalized volume of recipes. I honestly could not keep these kits in stock as they sold the moment I got them in!

There are not a lot of these kits available (some Hallmark stores, but not all, do carry them), which is why there is such a demand for them online. So, if you luck out and find these kits unused while out picking, snatch them up. Binder style books that allow you to add and delete pages are the most popular. However, bound book styles or those with plastic coil bindings will also sell.

While having an entire cookbook kit to sell will bring in the most money, you may find parts to these books that will also sell. For instance, the refill pages and extra recipe cards can sell on their own. Often people already have a book but need more pages or cards, and if the book is no longer being produced, they turn to Ebay to find more of these refills.

In addition to newer style cookbook kits, vintage recipe books are also popular, but only if they are new or just barely used (for instance, maybe only one page was written on, making it easy to tear out and then sell as unused). Any type of unused vintage recipe, address, baby book, or other scrapbook-type book is always an excellent pickup to sell on Ebay.

Note that because these cookbook kits are filled with blank pages that they cannot ship via Media Mail. Media Mail is for bound books that have actual written content inside. These kits, blank books, page refills, and/or recipe cards will have to ship via Parcel Post or Priority. Because they can weigh up to three pounds when packaged, these are an item I list with Calculated Shipping so that the buyer pays the postage cost to their zip code.

#59 MAGAZINE LOTS

Have you ever spotted a pile of magazines in the free box at a garage sale? Do you just toss your own magazines into the recycling bin when done reading them? Well, grab those free magazines and save up your own to resell on Ebay!

A lot of an entire year's worth of back issues is a popular way to sell magazines online, with niche titles such as those for particular sports or hobbies selling best. If you have several different magazines with the same famous celebrity on the cover, you can lot those together to resell. And there are some individual issues of magazines, usually a special edition or with a particular cover model that can sell on their own.

Save up your own magazines and then list an entire year's worth on Ebay; you may even earn back the cost of your subscription. Sites such as MySavings.com are always posting free magazine subscriptions, and some people subscribe to these strictly to resell them on Ebay, meaning they are actually making a profit off their free subscriptions!

Note that in order to ship magazines using Media Mail, they must be outdated, not current. Media Mail cannot be used to send magazines with current advertisements in them. For instance, if you have a magazine with a coupon in it that is still valid, that magazine cannot be shipped via Media Mail. Most magazine advertising is outdated after a year, so you can ship a lot of magazines from 2014, for instance, via Media Mail.

Magazine buyers on Ebay prefer magazines that do NOT have an address printed on them. I only resell magazines that ship to mean in plastic bags with my address printed on the outside (so that I can easily discard the bag) or with my address on a sticker that can be peeled off. Magazines need to be intact and like new in order to sell, so flip through any you pick up secondhand to be individual pages have not been ripped out and that there is not any damage.

Listing magazines on Ebay is easy as you only have to take one photo of the magazine's covers; to do this, I just spread out the magazine on a table and take one picture. In the listing, put the magazine title, the months/years included, and any celebrities who are on the covers (as the search feature can pick these names up). International buyers love to buy American magazines, so be sure to open up magazine listings to buyers outside of the United States using Ebay's Global Shipping Program.

When shipping magazines, do not just toss them into a box unprotected as they can get damaged during shipment. Remember that buyers want these magazines in excellent condition. Bundle the magazines together and wrap them in a few sheets of packing paper, and then use packing paper or peanuts to secure the bundle inside of the shipping box.

#60 MARY ENGELBREIT COLLECTIBLES

Mary Engelbreit is a popular brand of ceramics, books, housewares, and collectibles featuring funky, colorful designs, cartoon illustrations, and inspirational phrases. When I had my gift business, I used to carry Mary Engelbreit gift books, coffee mugs, and teapots; and I still look for them today when out picking as they remain excellent sellers.

Mary Engelbreit items are marked as such on the bottom of the pieces, and there is no knock-off market to worry about. These items are not too common, which also makes them more desirable on Ebay. And while Mary Engelbreit collectibles are not usually fast sellers, they are nice products to add to your inventory as they can draw traffic to your other listings.

Note that there are some older, retired Mary Engelbreit pieces such as certain dishes, cookie jars, and dolls that are extremely valuable, commanding up to $200 on Ebay. However, most items average between $20 and $50. In addition to everyday collectibles, there are also a lot of holiday-themed items under the Mary Engelbreit name. As with all collectibles, you should take some time to study the Mary Engelbreit "sold" completed listings on Ebay so that you know exactly what to look for when out picking.

And when you do find a Mary Engelbreit piece, be sure to turn to the "sold" listings again to see what the current selling price is. You will want to list these collectibles at Fixed Price so that you can get top dollar. If you do decide to list a piece at auction, make sure you start the

auction at the lowest price you will be happy with. I see many Mary Engelbreit items sell for only 99-cents as that was the starting bid, and only
one bidder came along.

Since Mary Engelbreit is a collectible, condition counts. Be sure to
check over the ceramic pieces for any chips or cracks. While having the
original box is nice, it is not necessary for the item to sell. These pieces
are very fragile and often times come in two or more pieces (such as
teapots and cookie jars with lids), so use plenty of bubble wrap and
packing paper. I list these items using Calculated Shipping so that the
buyer pays the postage cost to their zip code.

#61 MEN'S FEDORA HATS

It seems that every estate sale I attend has at least one pile of hats. While most are worthless on the resale market, one style I continuously am looking for is vintage men's fedora hats, which I always pick up if they are in good condition and priced for less than $5.

A fedora hat is defined as a fabric or wool hat with a wide brim and indented crown (top); the crown is typically creased lengthwise down the top of the hat and "pinched" near the front on both sides. The crown is usually around 4.5-inches tall, and the brim averages around 2.5-inches. Often a piece of ribbon trim is around the brim, and sometimes there is also a feather on the side.

If you plan to pick up hats to resell on Ebay, it is worth your time to study the various styles that are out there, and there are a lot. A Google search of "hat styles" will bring up numerous reference pages of hat pictures and names. If you sell hats on Ebay, trust me when I say you will be referring to these sites often as being able to provide the exact hat style name in your listing title will help sell your hat fast and for top dollar.

When selling any hat, it is crucial to provide the size. Most of the hats I find still have the original size tag inside, although sometimes they are missing. Running a tape measure around the inside brim will enable you to at least provide some sort of measurement in your listing. And even when there is a size tag inside, some customers will still ask you to give them a tape measure reading.

The more features a hat has (trim around the brim, a feather), the more money it will bring. I usually aim for a minimum of $25 for the nicest fedora hats I find. Condition is key with any hat you are selling on

Ebay; while I see many fedora hats while out picking, I end up having to pass on most of them as they are often stained or ripped.

While hats themselves are lightweight, their size can make it hard for them to fit in a standard shipping box. I often end up having to use the large 12x12x8-inch Priority Mail box to ship fedora hats in so that they can fit inside comfortably without the risk of being bent. We use some light packing paper or packing peanuts to give them extra protection during transit.

I always list hats at Fixed Price using Calculated Shipping so that the buyer pays the postage cost to their zip code. Hats can sell well internationally, so be sure to open up your listings to customers outside of the United States using Ebay's Global Shipping Program. Note that in order to ship internationally that you will have to use a plain cardboard box, not a Priority Mail box, and ship via Parcel Select. The package gets sent to Ebay's Global Shipping processing center, where the appropriate customs forms are attached. Ebay also assumes responsibility for the package if it is lost or damaged.

#62 MERRY MUSHROOMS CERAMICS

Merry Mushrooms was a line of kitchen décor and accessories produced by Sears Roebuck in the 1970s. Their orange, brown, yellow, and green designs are easy to spot, and people love their vintage, retro look. The most common Merry Mushroom items that you will find at garage and estate sales are the flour/sugar/tea/coffee canisters and the coffee mugs. There are also sugar and creamer sets, salt and pepper shakers, napkin holders, pots and pans, spice jars, and all sorts of dishes.

Authentic Merry Mushroom pieces are stamped with "Sears" or "Sears Roebuck" on the bottoms, as well as a made in Japan mark (sometimes you will see "Made in Japan," other times only "Japan." Most of the small items, such as the mugs, start at $10 on Ebay and go up into the $100 to $200 range for the rare dish sets and ceiling light fixtures.

The downside of these Merry Mushroom pieces is that they are incredibly fragile, so finding them without cracks or chips is challenging. I also find many that are stained; most were only lightly glazed with the coating not covering the entire piece, which then allowed food to get to the exposed ceramic. However, if you do find a set of canisters, for example, with condition issues on just one or two pieces, consider piecing them out as some buyers are only looking for a particular lid.

When listing Merry Mushroom pieces on Ebay, be sure to take pictures of all sides of each piece as well as a picture of the bottom where the mark is. There are some knock-off designs out there, so you want to be sure only to pick up and list the ones with the "Sears" and "Japan" marks. Also include the measurements as there were various sizes of these pieces (for instance, I have seen up to six different sized canisters), and you want to make sure customers know exactly what they are buying.

I actually prefer to piece these collectibles out as it makes shipping so much easier. I would much rather sell one canister for $10 than try to ship an entire set of four canisters in one box for $40. As I said, these pieces are very fragile, so take extreme care when packaging them. We tend to overpack these using a lot more bubble wrap and packing paper than we usually would.

As with most heavy items, I list Merry Mushroom pieces using Calculated Shipping so that the buyer pays the postage cost to their zip code. While I offer Parcel Post as the economy shipping option, I often upgrade the buyer to Priority Mail, which is not only faster but is also usually cheaper using my Ebay shipping discount.

#63 M&M'S COLLECTIBLES

Picking up M&M's merchandise to resell on Ebay can be tricky. While some pieces do well, there are many newer mass-produced items that won't bring you a penny. Every Christmas, there are a ton of M&M's gifts (coffee mugs, candy dispensers) filling the shelves at Target and Walmart, so serious collectors can easily find the products they want brand new. However, there are still M&M's collectibles that are worth picking up to resell on Ebay.

When it comes to M&M's collectibles, the overall condition, as well as the age of these pieces, is essential. The newer products (such as the novelty candy dispensers) are hard sells on Ebay, even new in the box as so many people now snatch these up on clearance to resell them online. I steer clear of the plastic candy dispensers that are dated from the past ten years.

However, there are plenty of other M&M's items that DO sell on Ebay, such as the large store displays, jumbo plush toys, figurines, Christmas displays, and Halloween scenes (especially if they were released under a brand such as Snowbabies or Danbury Mint), and Halloween costumes. And while the plastic candy dispensers are almost always worthless, note that there are earlier, much nicer machines that were produced, which are sturdy, well-made pieces with wood bottoms that can sell for upwards of $100 on Ebay.

Also, every year M&M's releases plastic Christmas and Easter tubes filled with candy that have an M&M's topper on them. While some of the older ones can sell on their own for a decent amount, if you have a lot of them, you can make even more. The average selling price for a lot

cxxxviii – #63 M&M'S COLLECTIBLES

of 20 of these toppers is $50, depending on the age, condition, and selection. Earlier ones had more bells and whistles with sound, movement, and/or lights; the newer styles tend to be just stationary figurines.

My rule when it comes to picking up M&M's products for Ebay is to check the date on the bottom of the piece to make sure it is not a recent release. A recent year along with a "Made in China" mark is always a good indication that the piece is mass-produced and not worth any money on Ebay. And while I will grab a newer M&M coffee mug if it is cheap, I do it more to bulk up the inventory in my Ebay store and to generate traffic to my other listings as opposed to expecting it to bring in much money on its own.

M&M's costumes are also great items to pick up, both in adult and children's sizes. You can usually find these gently used at garage sales for a dollar or two. Save any you find throughout the year and start listing them in August as people are now shopping earlier and earlier for Halloween.

#64 MODEL KITS

Putting together models may seem like an old-fashioned hobby, but there are still plenty of model kit enthusiasts out there today. If you have ever been to a hobby shop or craft store, you know how expensive these kits can be, which is why they are a smart buy at garage sales to resell on Ebay.

When I am looking at model kits to resell on Ebay, I make sure that even if the kit is opened that it is unused and that it was not even partially put together. If the box itself is not still sealed, sometimes the pieces inside are. It is important to make sure these sets are complete, so I do not advise buying them unless you know for sure that they are. Because I do not know much about model kits in terms of how they are put together, I only pick them up if they are new.

If a kit is extremely old or is a model that is highly desirable, you may be able to sell it if it is partially put together. However, it is essential that you accurately describe the pieces that are included and take lots of photos. Some vintage model kits can sell for hundreds of dollars to serious collectors, but those collectors are very particular about what they buy. Your best tactic for selling opened and partially assembled kits is to take plenty of photos of the contents and to sell them "as is."

While you do want to make sure any model kits you buy have all of the pieces included, if the paint has dried up, it can still sell. Most model kit collectors understand that paint dries out after a time, and since paint can be purchased cheaply at any hobby or craft store, not having it included with a kit is not a deal-breaker for buyers. In fact, if the paint in a kit I pick up is dried out, I usually just throw it away and then note in the listing that I disposed of it.

Some designer car model kits can sell for several hundreds of dollars on Ebay, and there are military aircraft models that sell for upwards of $200. If you have a smartphone with the Ebay App downloaded, it's easy to check on the "sold" completed listings for any models you find while out picking to see if they are worth buying to resell, along with how much you should pay to bring in a good profit.

#65 MUPPETS

The Muppets have seen a renewed popularity in recent years, although the merchandise is still relatively difficult to find. I always grab any Muppets items I see while out picking, of course, first making sure that they are in good, clean condition. Whether it is a plush toy or a coffee mug, a tie, or a novelty item, Muppets merchandise always does well on Ebay.

As with any licensed brand, the rarer the character, the more money it will bring. Gonzo is much more difficult to find than Kermit the Frog, for example. However, since it is challenging to find Muppets items anywhere new, most of the pieces tend to do well regardless of the character.

My most recent Muppet's find was a 3-ring binder from the 1980s that I got at a fill-a-bag estate sale. I quickly sold it for $10 on Ebay (Although I kind of wanted to keep it for myself as I had a similar one when I was growing up!). I have also sold Muppets men's neckties, plush stuffed toys, and figurines.

Note that there is a Muppets attraction at Walt Disney World in Orlando, Florida, at Disney's Hollywood Studios theme park, and there is a gift shop right next to the show. So, you may find Disney branded secondhand collectibles that were initially purchased at Disney. There have also been two new Muppets movies in recent years, and the Muppets television variety show is set to re-launch soon. So, there is newer merchandise out there with more likely to come.

In addition to plush toys, look for Muppets books, DVD's, playsets, puppets, lunchboxes, and figurines from the 1970s and 1980s, some of which can sell for hundreds of dollars on Ebay. The Muppets merged with Sesame Street several years ago, so it is not uncommon to now find co-branded Muppets and Sesame Street merchandise.

I always list any Muppets items on Ebay at Fixed Price as there are rarely two people on the site at the same time to engage in a bidding war if I list the item at auction.

#66 MUSICAL INSTRUMENTS & ACCESSORIES

If you have a child in band or orchestra or one who simply wants to TRY band or orchestra, you know how expensive musical instruments are to buy or even just to rent. Finding instruments in good condition secondhand for a reasonable price can be a challenge, but if you do, snatch them up as everything from guitars to flutes sell well on Ebay.

Even older musical instruments that are not in tip-top shape can sell online if they are vintage; however, unless you know a lot about the piece, these can be risky to pick up. Just because an instrument is old does not mean it has value, and often times these are priced high at garage sales and thrift stores because of their assumed worth. Add to the fact that picky collectors are the ones who buy these on Ebay, and you can quickly get in over your head trying to list them accurately and ship them safely.

However, if instruments are of interest to you and you are knowledgeable about them, then selling them on Ebay might be right up your alley. However, if you are not finding them at sales, consider placing an ad on Craigslist saying you buy used instruments. Many end up stuffed in a closet after a child quits playing it, so there are many out there. You just have to be creative in finding them. There is actually a man in my area who buys musical instruments to resell. He goes to every single garage sale in town and asks if they have any instruments they would like to sell.

If, like me, the idea of selling actual instruments is too intimidating, try looking for accessories such as straps, guitar picks, drum sticks, and foot pedals, carrying cares, and sheet music and songbooks. Not only are items like these often easier to find, but they are usually priced lower. I once picked up a vintage metronome (which is a device used to help pianists keep a steady tempo) at an estate sale for $5. It turned out not to be a valuable model (some can sell for hundreds of dollars), but it was still a quick and easy $30 sale on Ebay.

#67 NASCAR SPECIAL RACE SOUVENIRS

As a whole, I stay away from buying NASCAR items for resale on Ebay. The market is completely saturated with NASCAR diecast cars, shirts, and hats; so, most of the newer NASCAR branded items are worthless on Ebay. However, finding merchandise from select races and events CAN bring in money and are definitely worth picking up if the price is right.

Dated hats from races won by a particular driver, for instance, are usually good pick-ups as there was a limited number produced. Trucker style snapback hats indicated the hat has some age to it (as most newer hats are fitted), and this style of hat is extraordinarily collectible.

In addition to hats and souvenirs from dated racing events, I will pick up NASCAR jackets and coats if I can find them for a few dollars at a garage sale or the thrift store. Coats and jackets tend to be slower sellers, but eventually, they usually sell for around $50. As with all clothing, condition counts; so, before buying any hats or jackets to sell on Ebay, be sure to carefully examine the garment for rips or stains.

My rules when it comes to buying NASCAR items to resell on Ebay are to avoid anything that is currently being (or has recently been) sold at Walmart; only pick up newer items if they are in excellent condition; and stick to race event items, not basic driver-specific merchandise. I am also cautious not to overpay. Many people overprice these items at sales, so do not let yourself get tricked into thinking something will sell for a lot on Ebay just because the person selling it to you says it is valuable.

#68 NAVY SHIP SOUVENIRS

There are thousands of Navy ships, both currently in service and out of commission. Former sailors and their families love to find items from these ships, but there are not that many on the market. Therefore, when you do spot something with a United States Navy ship name on it, definitely pick it up to sell on Ebay.

The most common Navy ship items you are likely to find while out thrifting are baseball hats embroidered with the ship name. These are almost always mesh-style trucker snapback hats. Finding a hat from a ship that is no longer in commission is always a good item to pick up for resale on Ebay, but even hats from ships still sailing can sell. Often these items were either given to active duty sailors or were (and perhaps are still being) sold in Navel gift shops (such as the Pearl Harbor site in Hawaii).

In addition to baseball hats, look for vintage, original Navy hats and uniforms, postcards, prints, patches, and model kits, both assembled and new in the box. My dad served on the USS Norton Sound in the early 1950s, and I've picked up newly manufactured coffee mugs along with vintage matchbook covers for him with the USS Norton Sound name on them, paying as much as $25 for these small novelties.

While Navy ship souvenirs are usually inexpensive to pick up and make a fun addition to your Ebay inventory, they can take a while to sell as they have a small, niche market. So, you will need to be patient and wait for the right buyer to come along. These pieces are nice to have in your Ebay store, though, as they can bring traffic to the other items you are selling. Since you can usually find Navy souvenirs cheap, they are an easy way to beef up your listings.

#69 NEEDLEWORK & CROSS STITCH KITS

Even if you are not a crafter, you will want to educate yourself about needlework and cross stitch kits as they can sell very well on Ebay. I have found these kits at garage sales, estate sales, and thrift stores, usually brand new and priced for only a dollar or two. Kits that contain everything needed to complete a project are best, so make sure the kit includes a piece of fabric with the pattern, embroidery floss or thread, and instructions; all pieces should be detailed on the outside of the package, making it easy to double-check the contents if the package happens to be open (and sometimes the plastic on older packages splits open making these look as though they were used when, in fact, there were not).

I once bought a Snow White cross stitch kit in a bin at Goodwill for $1. It sold at auction on Ebay for $39! Looking back, I should have priced it higher at Fixed Price. While some vintage kits can sell for several hundreds of dollars, most sell in the $25 range. Many of these kits are Christmas themed, although there are some produced for other holidays such as Halloween as well as occasions such as weddings and new babies. And, of course, some are just general floral or other designs that can be displayed at any time.

These kits often produce a flat piece of work that can be framed; however, there are also kits for Christmas tree skirts, ornaments, and stockings. Dimensions and Sunset are two of the most popular makers of these kits, so remember those two names when you are out picking as they are usually the best quality kits to pick up.

Listing brand new needlework and cross stitch kits on Ebay is so easy; I just take a photo of the package's front and one of the backs of the package. I then copy everything that is written on the package into the listing (be sure to include the finished size piece the kit produces). Be sure to get a weight on any kits before you list them, as some do weigh in the one to two-pound range. I keep various plain bubble mailer envelopes on hand that these kits can easily slide into for shipment.

#70 NETWORK MERCHANDISE

I have talked a lot about television show and movie coffee mugs do-ing well on Ebay, but do not overlook network mugs and merchandise. Most of these items are only available at the stores at the network head-quarters or were only given to employees, making them hard for most people to get their hands on.

Unless you live in a city where a network is located (for instance, CNN is headquartered in Atlanta; so naturally, CNN merchandise pops up in Atlanta area thrift stores), you'll usually only find these items from someone who has visited New York or Los Angeles and purchased a souvenir at the studio gift shops. There is an NBC gift store in Times Square, and the television studios in Los Angeles offer tickets to live tap-ings of TV shows where merchandise is often sold. People go on vaca-tion, pick up a souvenir, and then end up putting it out at their next garage sale.

The last network coffee mug I sold was a CNN mug that I bought for 25-cents. It was a plain white ceramic mug with the primary CNN logo printed on one side, and it sold overnight for $9.99 (with the buyer paying shipping, of course). I have also done well with NBC snapback hats, especially NBC Sports. A good condition network cap can sell for upwards of $25 on Ebay (more if it is vintage with an older logo). NBC Sports Olympic branded items also do very well on Ebay.

#71 NICOLAUS COPERNICUS

Yup, here is another coffee mug to add to your list to be on the lookout for: Mugs featuring Nicolaus Copernicus sell well on Ebay!

Nicolaus Copernicus was a Renaissance mathematician and astronomer famous for making a model of the universe with the sun, rather than the earth, as the center. There is actually some merchandise relating to Copernicus out there, including coffee mugs. Ceramic mugs with a Copernicus theme are often sold in bookstores and museums and are an easy $20-$30 on Ebay, depending on the style.

In addition to coffee mugs, you may also find prints, postcards, stamps, and coins with Nicolaus Copernicus' image on them; although while some of these can sell for over $100, others are only worth a few bucks. Since I am not a paper or stamp expert, I only pick up these kinds of items is they are super cheap. However, I have yet to find anything other than Nicolaus Copernicus coffee mugs while out picking.

As with any collectible you pick up to sell on Ebay, the condition is important. When buying a ceramic coffee mug to resell, I take time to examine the piece thoroughly for any chips, cracks, or spoon marks (which are the scratches a spoon makes on the inside of mugs while stirring coffee or tea). Often Nicolaus Copernicus merchandise is branded with a bookstore or museum name.

To list a coffee mug on Ebay, I take pictures of it from all four sides as well as of the bottom and of the inside. I also list how tall the mug is in inches. Since mugs usually weigh in the one to the two-pound range when packaged for shipment, I always list them using Calculated Shipping so that the buyer pays the exact cost to have it shipped to their zip code. Most almost always fit comfortably into the 7x7x6 Priority Mail boxes that you can get for free from the Post Office, and we package them using plenty of bubble wrap and packing paper.

#72 NOVELTY CHRISTMAS STOCKINGS

If you have ever walked through the Christmas aisles at Target, Walmart, or department stores during the holidays, you have likely seen novelty Christmas stockings featuring cartoon and movie characters such as Disney and Star Wars. The price to buy these new is usually relatively high, which is why you should pick them up secondhand (or on clearance) to resell on Ebay.

If you do buy these Christmas stockings used, make sure they are CLEAN and in like-new condition. Most people actually plan to use these during the holidays, so condition counts. Many of today's styles come with plush character heads attached to the top. And some even light up or play music. Many sure the plush is clean and that any extra features are in working condition.

However, Christmas stockings do not have to be a recent release to sell on Ebay as vintage stockings featuring cartoon characters such as Peanuts and Garfield are also good sellers. In the case of a vintage stocking, a few small condition issues may not kill the sale as long as you disclose them in the listing. I've sold a Garfield stocking from the 1980s, for instance, that had a few faint marks on the felt.

I list these types of holiday novelties all year long as collectors are always picking them up and other customers shop for Christmas year-round. I always list these items at Fixed Price as it is rare that two interested customers will come along at the same time to start a bidding war.

While flat stockings are lightweight enough to ship in a bubble mailer via First Class Mail, note that the new styles with the plush details can weigh as much as two pounds shipped, so be sure to get a weight and build it into the price if you plan to offer "free" shipping; or else sell them using Calculated Shipping so that buyer pays postage.

#73 OPRAH WINFREY MERCHANDISE

Even though Oprah Winfrey no longer has her daily syndicated talk show, she is still as popular as ever! Her brand stretches worldwide, which is why merchandise featuring her name is in demand on Ebay. Most Oprah branded products are only available in her online store, and they are pricey new. So, picking them secondhand for a reasonable price is always a smart move.

One easy item to find is an Oprah tote bag, which many people get for free when they subscribe to her magazine. These bags are an easy $10-20 on Ebay. There are also Oprah branded coffee mugs, tee shirts, DVD's, Starbuck's tea, and even a line of Royal Copenhagen china dishes.

The only thing Oprah I generally stay away from are her books as they are so mass-produced and usually found in the clearance bins at book stores. However, a year's worth of back-issues of her magazine can sell for upwards of $30 on Ebay.

#74 PARIS THEMED DÉCOR

Paris themed décor has been popular for several years now. Even though it can be found at almost any discount store retailer, some of it can do well on Ebay. At a church sale, I was lucky enough to find a massive stack of metal Eiffel Tower centerpieces for $1 each. I snatched them all up, created one listing so that buyers could buy as many as they wanted, and priced them at $10 each. They all sold quickly and were easy to ship as they fit into the Priority Mail Shoe Boxes.

While I've found that Eiffel Tower tabletop statues are good sellers regardless of brand (the ones I picked up at the church sale had no branding on them), in general, when buying a home décor item to sell on Ebay, it's essential to look for a good brand as well as to scrutinize it for condition issues. I shy away from anything that is only stamped with "Made in China" as that is a clear indication it was mass-produced and sold in a discount or dollar store. However, some good brand names are made in China; so, if the brand is good, you can overlook the fact that it came from China.

Manufacturers are still churning out Paris themed pillows, clocks, dishes, nesting boxes, prints, signs, clothing, purses, and jewelry. These are typically items that you can pick up for cheap at garage sales as people who were once into the Paris-look want to switch up their décor. I only pick up décor items for a dollar or less, and I only list décor items on Ebay at Fixed Price as these products are not likely to inspire any bidding wars.

Note that home décor items are sometimes too big to fit into the Priority Mail boxes, so be sure you have a box before you list an item, so you will be ready when it ships. Home décor is another category where I list items using Calculated Shipping so that the buyer pays the postage cost. I simply weigh the item in a box on my digital scale and then put the pound range in the Calculated Shipping section of the listing (for instance, I listed the Eiffel Tower centerpieces in the one-to-two-pound range). I offer the customer both economy (i.e., slower) Parcel Select as well as expedited (i.e., faster) Priority Mail shipping. Most customers choose Parcel, but I am usually able to upgrade them to Priority as the Ebay online shipping discount makes Priority cheaper than Parcel in most cases.

#75 PATAGONIA CLOTHING

As I have said here and in my other books, there are thousands of clothing brands out there at garage sales and thrift stores; and the vast majority of them have no resale value on Ebay. However, one brand to always pick up is Patagonia! Patagonia is a California-based brand of high-end (i.e., high-priced) outdoor clothing for men, women, and children. Their winter parkas can sell as much as several hundred dollars on Ebay, although the average selling price for a men's Patagonia jacket is around $100.

In addition to outerwear, Patagonia also makes popular men's shirts, including Hawaiian prints. Some vintage Patagonia Hawaiian shirts sell for over $200, with more current releases selling for as much as $80. There are also Patagonia women's dresses, swimwear for men and women, and athletic wear.

I have found a few basic Patagonia men's shirts at my local Goodwill during their $1 sales, and they have all sold quickly on Ebay in the $30 range. Since Patagonia clothing is too expensive to be sold in the retail stores in the area I live in, I do not come across it often; but I always have my eyes open for it.

As with all clothing you sell on Ebay, the condition is vital. Be sure to check garments for rips or stains. I take pictures of the clothing from the front and back, as well as an up-close shot of the collar/tag area. And I take photos of special details such as buttons and pockets. With Patagonia, we sure to take a very clear photo of the label.

To sell clothing successfully on Ebay, you will need to provide accurate measurements. For shirts and jackets, I lay the garment on a flat surface and take three measurements: pit-to-pit (tape measure drawn from under one armpit across to the other); sleeve (tape measure drawn from the shoulder seam to the cuff; or from the collar to the cuff if there is no seam); and body length (tape measure drawn from the top of the shoulder to the bottom hem).

Patagonia shirts that are lightweight enough to ship via First Class get sent in poly bags. The jackets and coats, however, are usually too big to even be rolled up into a Priority Mail Flat Rate Bubble Mailer. So, for bulky pieces such as parkas, we wrap them up in packing paper before putting them into a large poly envelope.

Because the clothing categories on Ebay are so competitive, I list clothes with "free" shipping. However, shipping is never free as someone – the seller or the customer – has to pay for it. That is why it is important to have a digital scale so that you can weigh items before you list them in order to build the cost of shipping into the price of the item.

Because there are some Patagonia pieces that sell for hundreds of dollars, be sure to do a "sold" completed listing search to determine the value of any Patagonia clothing you want to sell. I like to price items slightly lower than the highest price listed on Ebay to ensure a fast sale. And for anything that sells for $100 or more, I pay to add insurance to the package, which is usually only a few dollars.

#76 PLAYING CARDS

Playing card decks are a dime a dozen, but collectible playing card decks are worth picking up to resell on Ebay. So, what makes a deck collectible? A deck that celebrates a special event or place is one thing to look for. Vintage sets with detailed artwork are another. Even a plain looking deck of sealed cards can be valuable if there are from a specific date or manufacturer or are co-branded. Some vintage playing cards and large lots of cards can sell for hundreds of dollars on Ebay!

Most people will price their playing card decks for a quarter at garage sales, and many estate sales just bundle them together for a dollar or two. If the cards look interesting and are in their original box, consider taking a chance and picking them up. Even a plain pack of Bicycle brand cards may be valuable if they are co-branded with an event or company.

Before listing opened packs of playing cards on Ebay, make sure all of the cards are intact, especially the Joker cards. Many sets are missing their Joker cards as people threw them away since they are rarely used in card games, which means there are people out there who only collect Jokers. I take a picture of the front and back of the card package; I also take pictures of the back of a couple of cards as well as a picture of all the Joker cards together.

And while some decks of cards can bring in big money, most sets I find sell in the $10 to $20 range on Ebay, which a bad profit considering they are so cheap to pick up! Double decks of cards in plastic cases with animal or flower designs are the ones I seem to find most often.

Note that some people are under the impression that because playing cards are paper, they can ship via Media Mail, but that is not the case.

Playing cards are NOT media and must be shipped via First Class, Parcel Post, or Priority. If you are selling cards in plastic cases, avoid putting them into bubble mailers to ship as you do not want to risk the breaking of the case.

#77 PLUSH TOYS

Plush toys are everywhere, from garage sales to estate sales. My Goodwill stores have huge bins filled with all kinds of stuffed animals. So, while finding stuffed animals is not a problem, finding plush that will resell on Ebay is a whole other issue.

When it comes to picking up plush toys to sell on Ebay, licensed characters and vintage pieces are ones to look for. Also, jumbo plush is almost always a great seller. However, regardless of age or style, the condition is what really counts. I only pick up plush if it is in good, clean condition. Hence, I do not go through the Goodwill bins as they are packed, and I am always worried about where the toys may have been in their journey from a home to the thrift store floor. With bed bugs having made a comeback in recent years, I am cautious about bring used stuffed animals into my home.

When I am at estate sales, however, I will look at any plush I find as most of the toys have been in storage inside of the home. I always keep an eye out for character plush from Disney, Peanuts, and Looney Tunes. In addition to making sure any plush, I am looking at it is clean, I also make sure all labels are still on, as many times people cut them off. Always be sure to look at the tag of any plush you find (it's usually on the rear end of the character) as sometimes a plain-looking stuffed animal may actually be a vintage treasure from a company such as Steiff, which can sell for thousands of dollars on Ebay.

If the piece is vintage and the original hangtag is still on it, I may overlook a small condition issue such as a bit of dirt. While you can wash most plush in the washing machine, vintage plush is much more fragile and can fall apart in the wash. We use Spray & Wash and an old toothbrush to spot clean any plush that needs it.

My favorite plush find was a giant stuffed Marmaduke dog that I paid $1.50 for at an estate sale. I then sold on Ebay for $40! Thankfully we had a huge box to ship him in!

#78 POLAROID CAMERAS & FILM

In my first book, "101 Items to Sell on Ebay", I talked about picking up vintage cameras for resale. To narrow down that category even further, always be on the lookout for Polaroid cameras and Polaroid film as Polaroid is a consistently good brand to sell on Ebay.

I still remember my family getting a Polaroid camera in the 1980s and how cool it was to see the photo come out of the camera moments after taking a picture and then watching as the shot developed! Since Polaroid has discontinued making these cameras, they are incredibly collectible.

There are lots of different styles of Polaroid cameras out there, some worth more than others, which is why I do not like to pay more than a couple of dollars for them. The One-Step cameras with the rainbow stripe on them, however, are particularly desirable; so, I will pay up to $5 for those models.

If I find lower value Polaroids that I can pick up cheap, I will save them up and sell them in a lot. But regardless of if I am selling one camera or a lot of 10, I sell all cameras "as is" as I have no way to test them. Camera collectors are incredibly picky about the items they purchase, so do not promise that a camera is in perfect working order unless you are absolutely sure it is.

While I list cameras "as is," I do make sure to take pictures of all sides of the camera as well as up-close shots of the mechanicals. I do a completed listing search for any camera I am selling and list it at Fixed Price using Calculated Shipping. Most cameras fit into the 7x7x6 Priority Mail box; we carefully wrap cameras in bubble wrap before putting them in the shipping box. And if the camera has any accessories, such as a flash, we wrap that piece separately.

Polaroid film that is still sealed is always a fast sell on Ebay, even if it is expired. I can often find new packages of camera film at estate sales for as little as a quarter. I then simply take a picture of the box or package, copy the information on the package into the listing, and include the expiration date. While I usually like to lot film together, Polaroid film will sell on its own. Some Polaroid film is so rare that several packages of it can sell for hundreds of dollars on Ebay!

#79 PORTMEIRION POTTERY

I have mentioned several times in my books about how I find table after table of pottery and porcelain at estate sales, most of it having no value on Ebay. However, there are some brands to be on the lookout for, one of which is Portmeirion.

Portmeirion is made in England, and they have produced an extensive range of both collectible and everyday dinnerware. Their Birds of Britain series is particularly valuable and can sell for hundreds of dollars on Ebay, but most of their pieces have floral or fruit designs. Portmeirion is clearly marked on the bottom of all pieces along with "Made in England." They have produced plates, bowls, mugs, and serving pieces.

As with any ceramic, condition for Portmeirion is critical. Before buying any piece of pottery, examine it thoroughly for any chips or cracks. I pass up any dishes that are damaged, even if they are a good brand name.

I have only ever come across one piece of Portmeirion in my time picking, a small teacup that I paid 25-cents for at an estate sale and sold for $10 on Ebay. Portmeirion continues to produce dishes, coffee mugs, and vases, and their coffee and tea sets are incredibly collectible. Even a set of four dinner plates sells on average for around $40 on Ebay.

The biggest challenge with selling pottery is shipping it. We use at least three sheets of bubble wrap between plates, and we use a lot of packing paper or peanuts inside of the shipping box. Pottery is another category that I list using Calculated Shipping so that the buyer pays the postage cost to their location. Again, having a digital scale makes this easy as you can weigh your item beforehand and then put the weight into the listing. Ebay's shipping calculator will then automatically figure the shipping total for the customer.

#80 PRESIDENTIAL MEMORABILLA

With every Presidential campaign and election comes memorabilia such as buttons, stickers, hats, shirts, and coffee mugs. While the candidate may not have gotten your vote, you will want to make sure to pick up any Presidential election items you may come across.

My favorite Presidential campaign souvenirs to pick up are, of course, coffee mugs! However, I also find a lot of buttons too. Hit up enough estate sales, and you will likely find election pins and stickers, usually priced pretty cheap. I have even found vintage ashtrays with the candidate's faces on them.

As with many small collectibles, I like to lot like items together for sale on Ebay. So, if I find several buttons from one candidate, for instance, I will just sell them all together. However, you can sell multiple candidate items together in a larger lot as many collectors are looking for any candidates, not just one. Not only do selling these items in lots make listing and shipping easier, but selling numerous items together tends to bring a better price than piecing each item out individually.

With collectibles, condition counts; avoid mugs with chips or cracks, and pass up paper that is torn or water damaged. Small Presidential election memorabilia does not bring in a huge amount of money, and customers are only after items in excellent condition. The exception to this is for vintage and antique items, especially from the 1950s or earlier, or if the candidate is extremely popular, such as Kennedy or Reagan. While a single Obama button may only sell for a few dollars, a Roosevelt button may go for several hundred.

#81 QUILTING SUPPLIES

Quilting is another popular craft that many people consider old-fashioned, but that has seen an increase in popularity in recent years. Quilting supplies are quite expensive new in the stores, so they are a great item to pick up at garage sales and thrift stores to resell on Ebay. Many thrift stores have bins dedicated to crafting supplies, so it is always worth your time to look through these bins for quilting supplies.

There are a wide variety of quilting supplies you will likely find at garage sales and thrift stores, with the fabric being the most common. Even a stack of fabric remnants can sell on Ebay, primarily if they are licensed character designs such as Disney or John Deere. Quilting is the art of putting different squares of patterns together so often, and people are looking for multiple designs in one lot.

Since I am not a quilter myself, I stick to picking up quilting kits. Some kits simply contain the pattern, while others also come with the backing and binding. And while some kits do come with all the fabric needed to complete a quilt, many quilting kits come with just one square, often called "Block of the Month" kits, with the quilter needing to buy multiple kits to complete a quilt.

Elaborate quilting sewing machines can sell for upwards of several thousand dollars on Ebay, although even small tabletop models can be worth a hundred dollars. These machines are often computerized so that they can be programmed to make whatever quilt design is entered into its system.

In addition to quilting kits, I have also had good luck selling hardcover quilting how-to books. These books are great to lot together; the last lot of three quilting books I sold went for $24.99, and I had only paid 50-cents for each of them.

Not sure you want to dive into the world of selling craft supplies on Ebay? Then skip the quilting kits and look for finished quilts, both handmade and manufactured. Finished quilted blankets, bedspreads, and pillows can all sell on Ebay if they are in good, clean condition and have either a designer brand name (such as Pottery Barn) or are of a vintage pattern (such as quilts made by the Amish).

If you do list a finished quilt on Ebay, be sure to take measurements and to take several photos of not just the front and back but also of the smaller patterns and squares. To take photos of blankets, I spread them out on top of a bed and back up in order to get the entire piece in the picture. I then edit any background items out so that buyers only see the quilt (not my bedside lamp!).

I usually ship quilting kits in a bubble mailer; note that these are sometimes too large to fit into the Priority Mail Flat Rate envelopes, so I actually have several other sizes on hand. I usually list craft supplies using Calculated Shipping so that the buyer pays the postage cost. To ship a finished quilt, we wrap it in packing paper and then ship it in either a box or a large poly bag via Parcel Post or Priority Mail.

#82 RAGGEDY ANN & ANDY

I still have my Raggedy Ann and Andy dolls from when I was a child, although the poor things are dirty and missing most of their clothing! There are Raggedy Ann and Andy collectors out there still, but not a lot of memorabilia, which is why if you do find something with Raggedy Ann and Andy on it, including the dolls, you will want to pick them up to resell on Ebay.

While there are some mugs, ornaments, and figurines featuring Raggedy Ann and Andy, the most common item remains the dolls. However, finding authentic vintage dolls in good condition can be a challenge. Many crafters have made knock-offs, so always be sure to check for a label on the doll (usually near their bottom) indicating that it is a licensed Raggedy Ann and Andy product.

The one exception to buying a doll that is not licensed is a handmade African American Raggedy Ann or Andy doll. A set of these can sell for up to $50 on Ebay.

A single vintage Raggedy Ann or Andy doll can sell for up to $80 on Ebay, depending on age and condition. A set of both dolls can sell for over $100. Many people sell the dolls together, but I feel you can get more for them if you sell them individually.

The Knickerbocker company held the license for Raggedy Ann and Andy, so you should see their brand on the label of most dolls you find. Also, look for a date, as the older the doll is, the better. Other brands that have had the Raggedy Ann and Andy licenses are Applause and Dakin, so you may occasionally see those brand names on the labels.

Raggedy Ann and Andy also have a camel named, strangely enough, "Camel with Wrinkled Knees." If you find one of these, either plush or ceramic, they go for as much as $60 on Ebay. You may also come across some Raggedy Ann and Andy bedding, party supplies, lampshades, and small toys and novelties.

Most Raggedy Ann and Andy items are vintage, and I always pick up anything that is vintage and licensed. Therefore, if it is in good condition and priced right, I always grab any Raggedy Ann and Andy items I find! I list Raggedy Ann and Andy items on Ebay at Fixed Price with Calculated Shipping; while they can be slow sellers, eventually, the right buyer will come along.

#83 REGIONAL RESTAURANT MERCHANDISE

If you have ever stopped at a roadside café or local restaurant, you may have noticed that some sell their own branded merchandise such as tee shirts and coffee mugs. If you come across these items (and it will usually be the mugs) while out picking, grab them if they are cheap as they can sell on Ebay.

I have sold ceramic and glass mugs from the Amish restaurants from the Amana Colonies here in Iowa, as well as mugs, steins, and shot glasses from eateries out of state that I have never heard of. People have favorite restaurants that are no longer open, or they always hit up a particular diner when on vacation. Buying novelties from these regional restaurants on Ebay is a way for them to hold on to those memories.

Besides coffee mugs and shirts, you may also find matchbooks, postcards, menus, and ashtrays. While you will not get rich selling regional restaurant merchandise, they are nice items to add to your Ebay store inventory as they can bring in traffic to your other listings. There are many buyers on Ebay searching for city and state collectibles, so I really like to add these products into the mix of items I sell.

#84 SAMSONITE TRAIN CASES

Nearly every estate sale I attend has a pile of old luggage, most of it unbranded or a discount brand, making it essential worthless to sell on Ebay. However, I always take a quick look to see if there are any vintage Samsonite train cases as these are hot sellers on Ebay! You may also luck out and find these at the thrift stores. My Goodwill stores pile their luggage under tables, so I often have to get down on my hands and need to sort through the bags.

When it comes to picking up train cases to sell on Ebay, what you want to look for are Samsonite hard case luggage, either boxy shaped with straight edges or with rounded edges. There are also pear or teardrop-shaped designs; these usually have straps for handles. Both the leather/wood and plastic cases sell on Ebay; a vintage set of cases can sell for over $200 hundred dollars depending on size, style, and condition.

And while the larger luggage pieces do sell, I prefer to stick to the small, easier to store, and easier to ship train cases; or makeup cases as they are also called. These pieces are the vintage versions of today's carry-on luggage and were used for toiletries, usually for women. These mid-century modern pieces of luggage were made in all shapes and colors, and they are highly collectible and sought after today as long as they are in good condition.

Finding these pieces of luggage in good shape, however, can be a challenge. Condition really counts when it comes to getting top dollar for these pieces. I have sold cases in the $30 range that would have gone for nearly $100 had they been in better condition. Often the inside mirrors are tarnished, the outside of the cases shows where there are stains on the inside, and the keys to the locks are missing. Each of these factors contributes to the value of the piece you are trying to sell.

The most common color you usually see in vintage Samsonite train cases is brown, either dark or beige; however, there were color models produced such as blue, pink, and red. These color pieces bring in the most money on Ebay. All Samsonite pieces are marked as such on the outside with a stamped metal logo.

When listing a train case for sale on Ebay, be sure to take pictures of it from all angles as well as of the bottom and inside. List any condition issues you see; also, be sure to disclose whether or not the keys to the lock are included, as well as if there is a mirror and/or a tray. Many of these came with a divided compartment tray that sits on the top of the opened case for storing small items, but I often find that the trays are missing or else cracked.

While the train cases are smaller than full-size pieces of luggage, they are usually too big to ship in a Priority Mail box. Therefore, be sure you have a plain cardboard box on hand for shipping. Due to their size and weight, these cases often need to be shipped via Parcel Post. I list them at Fixed Price based on the "sold" completed listings, and I list them using Calculated Shipping so that the buyer pays the postage cost to their zip code.

#85 SCHOOL DAYS PICTURE FRAMES

Here is another popular item I sold a lot of back in my gift business days: School Days Picture Frames! When I say "school days," I am talking about picture frames that feature a space for every grade, usually kindergarten through 12th. I used to carry a school bus shaped frame that I could not keep in stock as they almost always sold out as soon as a new shipment came in.

These novelty picture frames are the types of items you can usually find at garage sales as parents or grandparents buy them with every intention of putting their kid's pictures in them, but before they know it, the child has graduated high school, and the frame was never used. Therefore, it is not uncommon to be able to pick these up for a dollar or two.

I have found both ceramic and pewter school days frames; some have glass over the pictures while others have plastic. Some are shaped like school buses, while others are shaped like a school building. I can often fit these frames inside one of the Priority Mail rectangular boxes. While we carefully wrap all items we ship, be sure to take extra care shipping any picture frames with glass. For glass frames, we will use multiple sheets of bubble wrap and plenty of packing paper or peanuts to ensure the glass does not break during transit.

Condition is critical for picture frames as people are buying them to either display or give as gifts. I list all picture frames on Ebay at Fixed Price using Calculated Shipping so that the buyer pays the postage cost to their zip code. These school frames tend to sell best towards the end of the school year and then again at the beginning, and they also sell well during the holidays. However, I list them year-round as you never know who may be looking for one!

#86 SEED & FEED COMPANY BRANDED ITEMS

Agriculture is a massive part of Iowa's daily life and culture, so it is no surprise that I find seed as well as feed company-branded items at many of the estate sales I go to. For those of you unfamiliar with farming, "seed" is what farmers plant their crops with, while "feed" is what the animals eat. There have been dozens of different companies over the past one hundred years that have produced these farm staples, and their branded memorabilia sells very well on Ebay

When it comes to finding seed or feed company-branded items to sell on Ebay, trucker hats and nylon jackets are the most common items I encounter, with Pioneer brand being the most popular. However, I also find seed and feed bags, postcards, signs, brochures, and other novelties with seed or feed branded labels.

While Pioneer is the most common name to find, I also pick up a lot of Dekalb. However, there are many of these companies that have come and gone over the years; I will pick up anything seed or feed-related as the vintage pieces from businesses that no longer exist can be very valuable. Sometimes the item is obvious as to whether it is "seed" or "feed," while other times, there is just the company's name with some sort of farming graphic. A quick Google search will help you figure out precisely what the company produces so that you can properly list it on Ebay.

Ebay has an entire sub-category dedicated to "Seed & Feed Companies," which is located under the "Collectibles" main category (Collectibles – Advertising – Agriculture – Seed & Feed Companies). Some vintage pieces can do very well at auction as many farmers still prefer the auction format, so always check the completed listings to see how you should list any agricultural item you are selling.

My favorite seed and feed items I like to pick up to sell on Ebay are vintage trucker hats and nylon jackets. These either have patches sewn onto them or are embroidered with the company name and logo. Note that the patches alone have value, so do not hesitate to pick them up on their own or even remove them from hats or jackets that may have condition issues. If the jacket is torn but the patch intact, you can still make money from selling just the patch.

#87 SEWING BASKETS & BOXES

Sewing baskets and boxes, especially vintage ones filled with retro crafting goodies, are usually cheap to find at estate sales and easy to resell on Ebay. One of my favorite pickups was an adorable sewing basket from the 1970s that was originally sold at JCPenney's. It had all kinds of thread inside, as well as little sewing trinkets. I paid $1 for it and quickly sold it on Ebay for $30.

When buying sewing boxes to sell on Ebay, be sure to go through the contents (if there are any). You want to make sure another treasure did not get hidden inside that may sell on its own. I also like to clean these baskets out; if they have been in storage, it is not uncommon to find dirt or even dead bugs in the bottom.

You also want to gather up any sewing needles that may be in these baskets and tuck them safely in the sewing cushion or take them out altogether. You do not want an upset customer contacting you, saying they got stuck with needles when opening their package!

There are many different styles of these baskets and boxes, everything from large wood cases to baskets covered in fabric. A popular design is sewing baskets that resemble hat boxes; my mom used one of these in the 1970s, and I still have it today. Some of these can sell for upwards of $50 on Ebay, more if they are the hard-to-find pink color.

As with anything, people collect or plan to use themselves, and the condition is key when it comes to selling sewing baskets and boxes on Ebay. Ensure there are no cracks, that the interiors are not stained, and that the handles are intact. I mentioned dirt and bugs in cases that have been in storage but also check for mold. I've had to pass up many sewing baskets in my time as I find many that are just too damaged to be resold. It was that long ago that most women did a lot of sewing, so these baskets were heavily used.

Due to their size and weight, these baskets and boxes usually have to ship via Parcel Post, so be sure you have a plain cardboard box ready before you list one of these so you will be prepared when it sells. I list sewing baskets and boxes at Fixed Price using Calculated Shipping, with the buyer paying the postage cost to their location.

Do not just put a sewing basket or box into the shipping box unprotected; be sure to use plenty of bubble wrap, packing paper, and/or packing peanuts to protect it during transit. These vintage containers tend to be fragile and can crack if not appropriately packaged. We usually bag up any accessories inside of the basket, putting the bag back inside with packing paper around it. We then use more packing materials to protect the basket itself inside of the shipping box. The goal with all of this packing material is to prevent the basket and its contents from bouncing around while in transit. You want to be able to shake the box and not hear anything inside moving around.

#88 SHOT GLASSES

As a general rule, I stay away from glassware as most of it is worthless to list on Ebay. However, I will always take a look at any shot glasses I find, as some are collectible and will sell. In fact, there are vintage shot glasses that can sell on their own for hundreds of dollars; however, I usually find glasses that bring in around $10. Since I can often buy these for 25-cents, $10 is a decent profit.

I have picked up NBA, and NFL shot glasses for 50-cents and sold them anywhere from $5 to $10 on Ebay. Lots of shot glasses usually sell well if they are an entire collection or theme. I have also sold vintage shot glasses from closed Las Vegas casinos and torn down amusement parks. I will pick up any shot glass that is branded with a company logo, and, of course, vintage shot glasses are almost always a sure seller on Ebay.

I do not pick up shot glasses with cracks or chips; and, unless the glass is vintage, I also pass on ones where the graphics are fading. Most shot glasses do not have a maker's mark, only the logo design. Shot glasses are easy to list on Ebay as you only need a few photos of the glass from the front, back, and bottom. Putting a sheet of white paper in the glass will help you get a clear picture of the logo as the paper provides a solid background. I also list the height of the glass in the listing.

I only list shot glasses at Fixed Price; since they are so lightweight, I will usually offer "free" shipping on them. Single-shot glasses are light enough to ship via First Class; we keep various small boxes on hand just for these types of small items. I list most of the shot glasses I find at $9.99 with "free" shipping, which usually costs me around $2. And while the profit margin is not huge, these little glasses are so easy to list and ship that I do not mind adding them into my Ebay inventory. A small bit of bubble wrap and a little packing paper is all that is needed to ship shot glasses safely.

#89 SODA (DR. PEPPER, MOUNTAIN DEW, 7-UP) MERCHANDISE

Most pickers grab anything Coca-Cola or Pepsi-Cola related when out and about. In fact, in my first "101 Items to Sell on Ebay" book, I talked about how I prefer to pick up Pepsi items over Coke as they sell better. This is because Coca-Cola memorabilia has been so mass-produced in recent years that the collectible market has taken a hit. If I am faced with the choice of buying a Coke glass or a Pepsi one, I will always choose Pepsi.

In addition to Pepsi, however, you want to look for novelties from other soda brands such as Dr. Pepper, Mountain Dew, and 7-Up. There are not nearly as many of these branded items available, making them much more collectible, and therefore, much more valuable on Ebay.

One of my favorite finds was a lighted Mountain Dew sign that I got at a garage sale for $3. We spent $6 on a new light bulb for it and sold it promptly on Ebay for $40 with the buyer paying shipping. It was a plastic sign, too, not glass, which made shipping it a lot less stressful. I have also sold soda branded hats (the snapback trucker style with patches are the most desirable), nylon jackets, shirts (often from former delivery employees), pins, and bottles.

Vintage 7-Up glass bottles are also highly collectible depending on the year they were manufactured and their color. Since there are often boxes of dusty old soda bottles at estate sales, this is definitely an Ebay category you should take some time to study to educate yourself on what to look for. Some single vintage bottles sell in the $100 range, although, of course, many are worthless. It takes time and experience to pick the good ones from the duds.

#90 SNAPBACK HATS

There are a lot of baseball hats on the secondary market, but some have a unique appeal on Ebay: snapbacks! Snapbacks are essentially baseball-style hats with an adjustable "snap" strap in the back so that the size can be adjusted. So many of the hats that are produced today are sized and fitted, but many men prefer the one-size-fits-all styling of snapbacks. Plus, many have a vintage look that appeals to people over the new designs.

Trucker style snapbacks (the oversized gaudy ones that were popular in the '90s) have a considerable following, and collectors will pay big money for the ones with spray paint, graffiti design. Vintage sports team snapbacks from the NBA, NHL, NFL, and MLB are also extremely popular, with some styles selling for hundreds of dollars on Ebay. And of course, you cannot go wrong with licensed cartoon snapback hats from names such as Disney and Warner Brothers.

My absolute favorite snapback hats to find are one with Michael Jordan-era Chicago Bulls designs. I have sold a number of these in my years on Ebay for upwards of $50 apiece, and I was able to pick them up for a dollar or less. I also sell a lot of vintage John Deere snapback hats as well as hats with farming seed and feed logos on them. Any hat - sports, licensed brand, or otherwise - with a sewn-on patch is almost always a good pick up. Also, hats that have an embroidered logo or design on them usually mean they will be worth more than a hat with a simple screenprint design. If the tag inside of the hat reads "Made In USA," it is usually vintage as most hats these days are manufactured overseas.

I find many vintage snapback hats that have the foam linings rotted out of them; however, we simply clean the foam out and sell them as-is. It is also common to find these hats with sweat stains on the inside brim. By using some Spray & Wash and an old toothbrush, you can often get a lot of the stain out. You can also try hand washing snapbacks, but in general, you want to avoid putting them in the washing machine. However, gently stained hats can still sell; just make sure, to be honest about the condition in the Ebay listing and to take photos of any condition issues.

I have several hat forms (two pieces of plastic that fit around a hat to reshape it) on hand to straighten out misshapen hats. I also have a Styrofoam mannequin head that I purchased at Hobby Lobby that I use to model hats for photos. To list hats on Ebay, I take pictures of that hat from all four sides as well as the inside and, if I can, an up-close shot of the label. Most snapback hats are sized "one size fits all."

While hats are lightweight, do not make the mistake of putting them into an envelope to ship. You do not want to smash a hat down just to get it to fit into a shipping container. I find that many snapback hats slide easily into the Priority Mail Shoe Box size box, shipping for under one pound. It is a good idea to put a bit of packing paper inside of the hat so that when the buyer pulls the out of the box, it comes out nicely propped up.

#91 SNOWBABIES FIGURINES

While a lot of collectible figurines have no value on Ebay (think Cherished Teddies and Precious Moments), some Snowbabies will sell quite well. Snowbabies are little bisque figure "babies" in snow-like suits. There are single babies as well as those in elaborate scenes; some even have angel wings. While most are white, there have been some released with red "snowsuits." Snowbabies are sold at most Hallmark stores as well as at finer department stores and specialty gift shops.

Authentic Snowbabies are produced by Department 56, so be sure you find both "Department 56" AND "Snowbabies" marked on the bottom to ensure it is an officially licensed piece as there are many home-made crafted babies that look very similar but that have no value on Ebay.

There have been thousands of Snowbabies released over the years, so it is very common to see them sold at garage sales. However, it is also common to see these overpriced, at least in terms of picking them up to resell on Ebay. I come across many Snowbabies that are priced at $5 or more; however, I never pay more than $1 for them unless I am absolutely sure they are a valuable piece. Many of the basic Snowbabies only sell for around $10 on Ebay, but some can go for well over $100.

The most sought after Snowbabies are the ones that have been retired since around 2005. However, there are newer ones that only had a minimal release, making them extraordinarily collectible. Any Snowbabies that are co-branded with Disney are almost always going to sell well on Ebay. And the Snowbabies in the red snowsuits are also good to pick up.

Because there is such a wide value range with Snowbabies, they are an item I do like to look up before buying. While I do not like to rely on my smartphone while out picking, I will use the Ebay Mobile App to look at the "sold" completed listings on any Snowbabies I am unsure about.

Having the original box for any Snowbabies you are selling on Ebay is nice but not always necessary. Some Snowbabies are very elaborate and detailed, which can make shipping them a challenge. Having the original box with the fitted Styrofoam inserts helps significantly as they were designed to protect the specific piece. I've wary of picking up any of the larger Snowbabies that do not come with boxes as the risk of them breaking during shipment is very high. When we do ship Snowbabies without their original boxes, we take great care to protect them with a lot of bubble wrap and packing peanuts.

#92 THEME PARK SOUVENIRS

In the first volume of my "101 Items to Sell on Ebay" series, I talked about picking up Disney theme park merchandise. However, I advocate snatching up items from any amusement park, whether it is from Universal Studios or the park in your area. Since theme park merchandise is usually only available at the actual park and not even sold by the company online, people turn to Ebay to find these souvenirs.

Finding vintage items with older logos or souvenirs from parks that are no longer open will almost always result in an Ebay sale as people look to recapture their childhood memories. In Iowa, we have Adventureland Park, and I have sold several items (including mugs!) that I have found secondhand. I have also picked up items from Great America and Six Flags, all of which have sold well and relatively quickly on Ebay.

In addition to coffee mugs, most theme parks sell hats, tee shirts, plush toys, and all sorts of small novelties. I have sold theme park shot glasses and buttons, as well as old park maps and brochures. I sell a lot of Disney and Universal Studios tee shirts, which I find all the time at thrift stores for as little as $1.

While theme park souvenirs may not bring in the big bucks, they are cheap to buy, easy to list and ship, and generally sell fast, making them great items to add to your Ebay inventory mix. And Disney items, especially, can help to draw in traffic to your other listings as many people are searching for anything Disney online. So, while they may not end up buying your Disney item, they might find something else that catches their eye!

#93 THOMAS KINKADE

"The Painter of Light," Thomas Kinkade, passed away in 2012, which has made his already expensive pieces even more valuable. Most people know of his paintings, but he has a wide range of licensed merchandise on the market, including mugs, figurines, and holiday decorations.

I was at an auction not too long ago where I was able to get a Thomas Kinkade light-up table-top Christmas tree for only $1. It worked, but was missing the cord needed to connect it to other pieces; plus, the plaque on the front of it was scratched. It would have sold for over $100, but I was still able to get $50 for it!

Thomas Kinkade framed artwork can sell for thousands of dollars, but there are also plenty of his pieces that only go for a few hundred dollars, some even less. And buying artwork to resell on Ebay can be tricky. For one, you have to be educated about spotting potential fakes. And two, you have to be able to ship what is usually a large, heavy piece.

I prefer to stick to picking up the home décor, gift, and novelty items that have been released under the Thomas Kinkade name. Not only are these products not subject to counterfeiting, but they are much easier to list and ship.

The Bradford Exchange has produced several Thomas Kinkade collectibles over the years, including the Christmas tree I mentioned as well as Christmas village houses, ornaments, music boxes, and even jewelry. There are also Thomas Kinkade Disney canvas prints and puzzles. These smaller Thomas Kinkade collectibles sell for as little as $10 all the way up to over $100, so be careful about overpaying. And when you do list anything Thomas Kinkade on Ebay, do it at Fixed Price as these items do not usually bring in bidders when listed at auction.

#94 TUPPERWARE TOYS

If you were a child of the '70s or '80s and your mom attended Tupperware parties, she may have brought you home a Tupperware toy. The most famous Tupperware toy is the Shape-O ball, a plastic ball with cutouts that you put plastic shapes through. There are also other toys, including playsets. I myself had the Mini Mix It kitchen set, which I used to make Play-Doh cookies!

If you hit up enough garage sales, you will likely come across quite a bit of old Tupperware. And where there is a lot of adult Tupperware, you can usually find some of the toys. The key to selling any Tupperware, including the toys, is condition. For the playsets and cooking sets, having the original box is crucial to getting top dollar.

However, while Tupperware toys are well made and do sell on Ebay, they are not big sellers. Usually, vintage toys bring in quite a bit of money online, but the Tupperware ones tend to top out in the $50 range. And that price is reserved for huge lots of toy Tupperware play dishes. While the Mini Mix It kitchen set may bring in $30 if in mint condition in the original box, other items may only sell for a few dollars.

I myself have sold the 1989 Playground set for $25 (I paid $1). It had all the pieces, was in excellent condition, and came with the box. However, I have picked up other Tupperware toys that had no resale value on Ebay. Your best bet when picking up Tupperware toys is to only buy those in like-new condition and to never pay more than a few dollars. If you come across a box of the play dishes, note that those sell well as a lot. All Tupperware is marked at such on the bottom, making it easy to identify.

#95 VINTAGE HANDBAGS

I have talked about my love of estate sales (in fact, I pretty much buy most of what I resell on Ebay at estate sales and rarely go to garage sales), and I especially love ones full of vintage clothing and accessories. I am not an expert on vintage clothing, but one item I will pick up if I can find it in good condition are vintage women's handbags.

There are so many cheap bags being produced today, so finding an authentic vintage bag is a real treasure hunt. The first clue to whether a bag is vintage is to look inside for a tag. If the label reads "Made in China," walk away as that is a clear indication the bag is not vintage. If you cannot find a label, look carefully at the lining. Is the stitching off? Is the fabric itself a starchy polyester? Is there any plastic on the handle or closure? Mass-produced features such as these are another sign a bag is likely modern and not vintage.

I look for vintage handbags with unique features such as beading, jeweled handles, and patent leather shells. Most vintage bags are small as they were carried as clutches. Those with handles tend to feature delicate chains. Many of these older bags do not have a brand label inside, but with time you can learn to spot the vintage bags from the newer styles.

While some stains on the inside lining of a vintage handbag can be expected (usually from old makeup), a bag that is clean with no tears and an intact strap is a safer bet. Since value can vary widely, I never pay more than a couple of dollars for any bag. These types of purses, especially ones that are unbranded, can do well in lots as women are looking to add several pieces at once to their handbag collections.

Depending on the style, size, condition, and whether or not there is a brand label, I price vintage handbags anywhere from $15 to $50. Since it can be hard to find the exact same bag in the completed listing search, I often have to go on instinct when pricing vintage bags.

To list a vintage handbag on Ebay, I take pictures of the front, back, and inside. I provide the measurements in inches of the width, depth, and length, as well as the strap drop (the measurement of the handle from the top of the bag to the height of the strap). I list all handbags at Fixed Price, and if they are lightweight enough to ship in a polybag via First Class, I usually offer "free" shipping, building a few dollars into the asking price to cover the cost of postage.

#96 VINTAGE HAWAIIAN PRINT CHILDREN'S LUGGAGE

I didn't get to visit Hawaii until I was in my 30's, but I still had a cute little Hawaiian print suitcase as a child! Surprisingly, these bags sell for around $25 on Ebay, so if you find one for a dollar or two that is clean and in good shape (and the condition is critical with these; pass up any that are dirty or torn), be sure to grab it.

These suitcases are easy to spot as they have wild, colorful floral patterns. They were made in the 1970s, so they definitely have a late 60's, early 70's hippie-style look to them. They are made of fabric, so they are relatively lightweight for luggage. There is one main zippered compartment, although some have a snap pocketed pouch on the outside.

As with most luggage, these suitcases also originally came with a little lock and key. Having the original lock and key for any piece of luggage you are selling on Ebay is always a plus; if they are not on the outside attached to the zipper pull, check the inside pouches as they may have been tucked in an interior pocket.

The only downside to selling any piece of luggage, including these smaller Hawaiian suitcases, is that they can be challenging to ship. Even though they are child-size, these do not fit in most standard shipping boxes, so be sure you have a shipping box ready before you even list a bag so you will not be scrambling for a box when it sells. My dad usually has to craft a box for large, oddly shaped items such as these suitcases. He keeps a wide variety of cardboard scraps on hand just for this purpose.

cciv – #96 VINTAGE HAWAIIAN PRINT CHILDREN'S LUGGAGE

Because of their size, these suitcases need to be shipped via Parcel Select. While we do wrap everything we ship before putting it into a box, you do not have to go overboard with packing materials around these suitcases since they are fabric and a bit soft and not prone to breakage.

#97 VINTAGE FASHION DOLL ACCESSORIES

Everyone knows about Barbie dolls, and most people know that vintage Barbie dolls and accessories sell well on Ebay. However, in the 1970s and 1980s, other companies produced doll accessories to fit Barbie that were not Mattel or Barbie trademarked. And these pieces, even though they were not produced by Mattel or Barbie, can still sell well on Ebay.

One such company that made 11-inch doll furniture in the '70s was Wolverine. I found a Wolverine Wardrobe new in the box at an estate sale. While everything else at the sale was out of my budget, this toy was only $1. Unfamiliar with it, I took a chance, bought it, and listed it on Ebay, where it quickly sold for $20!

In addition to general doll furniture, Wolverine also held the license for Rainbow Brite toy kitchens. While they produced larger metal dollhouses and kitchen sets, their Barbie-sized pieces were made of plastic.

Other vintage clothing, accessories, and furniture were also produced to fit 11-inch dolls such as Barbie. In addition to plastic pieces, some were made of wood or were even inflatable. As with any item, the true test to see if a piece is vintage is to look for a "Made In" stamp on the bottom or back of the pieces. If it reads "Made in China," it is NOT vintage. There are many knock-off Barbie toys still being produced today that are sold at dollar stores, so take the time to look for marks to indicate whether or not a piece is truly vintage.

Also, be aware that putting "Barbie" in the title of a listing that is NOT for a licensed Barbie product is called keyword spamming, which directly violates Ebay's policies. Keywords to use, instead, are "vintage 11-inch dollhouse furniture".

#98 WOMEN'S MALL BRAND CLOTHING

As I have talked about several times, clothes are a dime a dozen at thrift stores and garage sales; and the vast majority of clothing has no re-sale value on Ebay. Usually, it is only vintage pieces, designer brands, and plus size garments that will sell online for a reasonable price. However, while they will not make you rich, there are some standard mall brands of women's clothing that can do well on Ebay; and the bonus is they are usually cheap and easy to find secondhand.

Clothing from stores such as Chico's, Coldwater Creek, Eddie Bauer, and Talbots are usually good pieces to pick up, selling on Ebay for an average of $25. These stores are in many large shopping malls, making their clothing easier to find at garage sales and thrift stores in most parts of the country. Even clothing from more mid-priced stores such as Christopher & Banks, CJ Banks, and Dress Barn can sell for an average of $20 on Ebay, depending on the style.

As with all clothing, condition and size are important, as is the uniqueness of the garment. I can get more for a Chico's denim jacket than a basic knit top, for example. I am able to buy clothing for as little as $1 during a Goodwill sale, and I stick to the coats, jackets, and women's blazer sections to find pieces that I can sell for at least $20 on Ebay. It is not at all unusual for me to buy a cart's worth of these mall brands during one trip to Goodwill. Since high-end designer clothing is not sold here in Iowa, I am thankful to at least have these moderately priced pieces to make money on. And since they do not sell for hundreds of dollars, I also do not have to deal with the customer complaints and returns that often accompany selling high-priced items.

Modern clothing from mall brands must be in excellent condition to sell on Ebay, so be sure to check pieces over thoroughly for rips or stains. Larger sizes always sell better than smaller ones in most brands, but I have sold small size women's jackets from Chico's, Coldwater Creek, Eddie Bauer, and Talbots for as much as $40. I stick to coats and jackets sized large and up from Christopher & Banks. CJ Banks is Christopher & Banks plus-size sister store, so all of their pieces are sized extra-large and up.

To sell clothing successfully on Ebay, you will need to provide accurate measurements. For shirts and jackets, lay the garment on a flat surface and take three measurements: pit-to-pit (tape measure drawn from under one armpit across to the other); sleeve (tape measure drawn from the shoulder seam to the cuff; or from the collar to the cuff if there is no seam); and body length (tape measure drawn from the top of the shoulder to the bottom hem).

Take photos of clothing from the front and back, along with an up-close picture of the tag. I list all clothing at Fixed Price, and because the clothing categories on Ebay are so competitive, I list clothes with "free" shipping. However, I figure out the shipping cost before listing an item and then build it into the asking price. If I think a jacket is worth $18 and will ship in a Priority Flat Rate Envelope for $5, I will list it for $24.99 with free shipping.

#99 WORLD BANK GLOBES

Once at an auction, I bought a box of random vintage items for $3. A man quickly came over to me, offering me $2 for a little metal globe that was inside. I said no, figuring if he wanted it that it must be unique. The globe was a World Bank Globe with "As You Save So You Prosper" on it, and it was made by the Ohio Art Co. I put it up for auction on Ebay, and it sold for $10. While it was not a big profit, it was easy to list, easy to ship, and it sold fast.

There are many different styles of these little bands, some with more details and colors than others. The average selling price is around $20, although some can go for a few dollars more. The key to selling these little banks on Ebay is finding them in good condition as they are often rusty, dented, or have missing pieces. The condition must be very good for these to sell, so pass up any significant damage.

Small items such as these globes are lightweight enough to ship via First Class mail, so make sure you have a little box on hand for shipping. The first Ohio Art globe I sold I put up at auction, hence why I only got $10 for it; now I know better and list these at Fixed Price at the price I want.

#100 YANKEES JACKETS

I am not a baseball fan, but nothing gets me more excited than finding a vintage nylon New York Yankees jacket! I was lucky enough to stumble upon a garage sale where I found THREE for only $2 each. I quickly sold them on Ebay for a whopping $50 apiece!

These nylon jackets feature embroidered Yankee logos on the front and back and usually have snap fronts. Their insides are often lined with a thin cotton fabric, and the labels indicate they are vintage if they are marked as "Made In USA." Not only will adult Yankees jackets sell, but so will youth sizes. Since people are buying these to wear, the condition is important; so be sure to check for stains or rips before buying them to sell on Ebay.

As I have said several times already, to sell clothing successfully on Ebay, you will need to provide accurate measurements. For jackets, lay the garment on a flat surface and take three measurements: pit-to-pit (tape measure drawn from under one armpit across to the other); sleeve (tape measure drawn from the shoulder seam to the cuff; or from the collar to the cuff if there is no seam); and body length (tape measure drawn from the top of the shoulder to the bottom hem).

Take photos of these jackets from the front and back, along with an up-close picture of the tag and all of the embroidery. These jackets can be rolled up and mailed in a Priority Mail Flat Rate Bubble Mailer for under $6.

I am not quite sure what is so special about these jackets, but the Yankees do seem to have a very loyal fan base. And since these jackets sell so well, I do not question their loyalty!

#101 YARN & KNITTING SUPPLIES

I estimate that half of the estate sales I go to have yarn and knitting supplies, and I always give them a look to see if they are worth picking up to resell on Ebay. First, I check the packages of yarn to make sure they do not have 99-cent stickers on them. After all, yarn is sold at Walmart; most people do not come to Ebay to buy what they can get at their nearby big box store. Often entire bags of yarn will be priced at only a few dollars at sales. However, most yarn I find is partially used; and since I am not an expert on yarn, I only buy new packages.

I focus on the higher-quality yarn that I can resell in bundles. Yarn made from cotton or wool (especially cashmere) is much more valuable than acrylic. However, if you find a considerable lot of new yarn in one pattern or color, you will likely still be able to sell it even if it is acrylic. Multi-color yarn is also a good pick up regardless of what it is made of.

Finding packages (or "skeins") of yarn all in the same color is most desirable as people are looking for enough yarn to complete projects such as sweaters and blankets. They are also looking for colors and patterns that have been discontinued. And while selling yarn in lots of the same color is the most popular way to list it on Ebay, you can also sell lots of multiple colors. The key with selling yarn on Ebay is having several skeins in one listing; so, lots are the way to go.

In addition to yarn, pattern books and knitting needles will also sell on Ebay. These items are pretty easy to find secondhand, so do not hesitate to grab them when you find them cheap and in good condition. Knitting and crochet books can ship via media mail, while skeins of yarn are easy to bag and ship in a large box or in a large poly bag.

You do not have to understand the craft of knitting to sell big lots of yarn on Ebay. It is easy to find, easy to list, and easy to ship!

CONCLUSION

So, there you have it: 101 MORE items that you should be able to easily find secondhand to resell on Ebay! If you haven't already, be sure to check out the first book in this series, "101 Items to Sell on Ebay: How to Make Money Selling Garage Sale & Thrift Store Finds!" Between that book and this one, you will have a huge list of 202 things to look for while out picking that can make you money on Ebay!

As much as I stand behind the items listed in this book, remember, too, that a lot of things can factor into a successful Ebay sale. Your feedback rating, quality of photos, shipping charges, item condition, competition, and current demand all determine the price you will get. Before listing any item on Ebay, be sure to do a completed listing search to see what the going rate for yours is. While these are my own personal success stories, what sells today may not sell tomorrow as the Ebay market is continually changing.

Selling on Ebay, while fun and profitable, is work. The harder you work, the more money you will make!

ABOUT THE AUTHOR

Ann Eckhart is an author, reseller, and online content creator based in Iowa. She has written numerous books about how to make money online from home. You can keep up with her on her website at www.AnnEckhart.com as well as on social media:

Facebook @anneckhart
Twitter @ann_eckhart
Instagram @ann_eckhart
YouTube @seeannsave

CPSIA information can be obtained
at www.ICGtesting.com
Printed in the USA
BVHW041544100821
614092BV00014B/1187